California's El Camino Real
AND ITS HISTORIC BELLS

Max Kurillo and Erline M. Tuttle

Published in cooperation with

the California State
Automobile Association

and with

the Automobile Club of
Southern California

WE'RE ALWAYS WITH YOU.®
——— 1900·2000 ———

Sunbelt Cultural Heritage Books
"Adventures in the Natural and Cultural History
of the Californias"
A series edited by Lowell Lindsay

SUNBELT PUBLICATIONS
San Diego, California

EL CAMINO REAL
MISSION SAN GABRIEL 9 M.→
← MISSION SAN FERNANDO 23 M.

Copyright © 2000 by Sunbelt Publications, Inc.
All rights reserved. First edition
Editing, design, and composition by Lynne Bush
Printed in the United States of America

No part of this book may be reproduced in any form without
permission of the publisher. Please direct comments and inquiries to:

Sunbelt Publications, Inc.
P.O. Box 191126
San Diego, CA 92159-1126
(619) 258-4911, fax: (619) 258-4916
www.sunbeltpub.com

04   03   02   01   00   5   4   3   2   1

Library of Congress Cataloging-in-Publication Data

Kurillo, Max. 1930-
    California's El Camino Real and its historic bells/Max Kurillo and Erline M.
    Tuttle.
        p. cm.
    ISBN 0-932653-37-5
    1. El Camino Real (Calif.)-History. 2. Bells-California-El Camino Real.
    3. Historical markers-California-El Camino Real. 4. Historic sites-California-El
    Camino Real. 5. Missions, Spanish-California-History. 6. California-History-to
    1846. I. Tuttle, Erline M. 1931-. II. Title.
    F864.K87 2000
    979.4-dc21   00-032232

Credits: Unless otherwise noted, all documents and photographs courtesy
of Kurillo/Tuttle Archive. Strip maps of El Camino Real from the 1912
Tour Book, courtesy of American Automobile Association. Illustrations on
title and contents pages from the stationery of Mrs. A. S. C. Forbes,
Kurillo/Tuttle Archive.

DUX FEMINA FACTI

(Feminine leadership has accomplished it)

ഇ⊃Cദ

Dedicated to the women who preserved and
marked El Camino Real of California

Contents

Foreword   vii
Preface   ix
Acknowledgments   xi

THE HISTORIC CORRIDOR   1

The March to Alta California   8

El Camino Real in Alta California   11

Branches of El Camino Real   13
Routes North   15
Alternate Routes of El Camino   19
    Real

THE ROAD   21

El Camino Real in Transition   25

The Stage Era   26
From Trail To Road   27
The Good Roads Movement   31
Adventure or Nightmare?   32
The Transition Continues   37

Saving El Camino Real   39

A Little White Line   44
The State Historical Landmarks   46
    Commission

THE BELLS   49

The Birth of an Idea   53

A Statewide Project   54
The Project Begins   56
The Los Angeles Convention   57
The Santa Barbara Convention   59
Funding the Project   60

Tracing the Route 63
Designing the Bells 63

The Bells Become a Reality 67

Casting the Bells 69
Mystery Bells 73
The Cost of the Bells 74
Maintaining the Bells 75
Locations Beyond El Camino 77
Real
The UCB Bells 79

The Adopt-A-Bell Project 81

El Camino Real and the Bells of 85
Ventura County

El Camino Real in Ventura 89
County
The Dedicated Women of 96
California

APPENDIX 97
The Route of El Camino Real, circa 1900 99
American Automobile Association Strip Maps of 101
El Camino Real, 1912
Generations of El Camino Real Bells 110
Donors and Locations of Bells 117
Bells Donated by the California Federation of 125
Women's Clubs
Biographies
Mrs. A. S. C. Forbes 129
Justin Kramer 135

Foreword

ઠ૭Ͼ𝔢

If one were asked to provide a symbol for California, chances are quite good that El Camino Real, the Royal Road, would be selected. But doesn't "El Camino Real" refer to a trail established by the Spanish Crown? Indeed it does. California was at one time a part of New Spain. At the same time that our founding fathers on the East Coast were establishing a new nation, the United States of America, the Spanish Crown was establishing a foothold in California to thwart the Russian invasion from the north. A route of communication had to be built to establish continuity from what is now the Mexican border to the northernmost point of Spanish rule, first to Monterey and finally to Solano in present-day Sonoma County. Franciscan friars, inspired by the legendary Padre Junípero Serra, took advantage of the route by establishing missions along it. The missions are now world-famous landmarks of California.

At the turn of the century, the importance of El Camino Real as part of California's history came to be recognized, and markers were placed along its route. When the automobile arrived, El Camino Real entered a new era. My grandfather once traveled from Ventura County to Orange County on El Camino Real. Automobiles were not numerous at the time, but there were enough to scare my grandfather's horses. The automobile was here to stay, however, and so was El Camino Real.

My association with El Camino Real only began recently when my bell design became the bell of choice for those placing the well-known markers along El Camino Real. It has been a privilege for me to be associated with that project since 1960.

The authors of this book have left no stone unturned in tracing the history of El Camino Real from the time when the Spanish army crossed over the border from Baja California to Alta California in 1769 to the present. They have meticulously searched records, inspected surveys, and interviewed countless people. The story they tell begins not just at the border between Baja California and Alta California but traces the origins of El Camino Real in old Spain. They have visited many sites that are virtually unknown today but are an important part of the story. Their painstaking work is a real contribution to understanding present-day California. Our chapter, the present, cannot be fully appreciated without knowing what happened in the past, at the beginning of El Camino Real.

Justin Kramer
January 1, 2000

Preface

We wish to make it clear at the outset that this book is not intended to be a complete history of El Camino Real. Rather, it is the story of the great movement of a number of California women's clubs to save the most historic road of the Californias. It is also the history of the roadside markers, the El Camino Real bells, and of the early organizations responsible for placing the bells, as well as those groups still active today. Each has its own unique history, which we offer to you as it has been supplied to us by these organizations. The listing of bell locations, confusing as it may seem, is an integral part of the history, but is only as good as the information provided. Many organizations report yearly, but the reports are often insufficiently detailed, with general statements such as ". . . placed eight bells this year." We regret that the data given is often insufficient to give these organizations proper credit. We have done our best to check the information we have and apologize for any omissions or errors.

In this revision, we hope to present an authoritative popular history. Since it is intended for the general public, we omit much of the detail of El Camino Real routing through present-day communities, with the exception of Ventura County, which we present as an illustration.

We felt the time had come to revise the original *Marking the Past* because of the tremendous amount of new activity since its first publication. The club women of California have, once again, put forth a heroic effort. Their story needs to be retold.

It could not have been possible, at the dawn of the movement to save El Camino Real in California in 1892, for anyone to anticipate the sheer amount of work that would ensue over the years. The establishment of these roadside markers has been, overwhelmingly, the work of the "women of California." Although their dedication to the project of marking El Camino Real of California faltered during dark times in our nation's history, it has always rebounded with renewed fervor.

In recent years this ambitious project has been accelerated and has even extended southward, marking El Camino Real in the two states of Mexico, Baja California and Baja California Sur, as well as in Alta California. This accomplishment alone has made history in two sovereign nations, uniting two peoples with a common heritage and shared cultural history in friendship. We hope to celebrate the accomplishment of these women, organized in a common cause. It is truly astounding; and still they work on.

Max Kurillo
Erline M. Tuttle

Acknowledgments

The authors wish to thank Charles Johnson, Ventura Historical Society; Maureen Everett, California Federation of Women's Clubs (CFWC); Katherine Toner (CWFC); Mary Louise Days, historian for the Native Daughters of the Golden West (NDGW); Native Sons of the Golden West (NSGW); Dottie Goldbeck; Dr. Israel Barken; Monsignor Francis J. Weber; Morgan P. Yates, Automobile Clubs of Southern California (ACSC) Corporate Archivist; Don Patton, Justin O'Brien and Alison Moore, representatives of CSAA; Jim Larson, Kyle Nelson, Steve Saville, Olga Estrada, Marlene Davis, Carmen Mullenix, and Vince Meneses of San Diego District 11 Caltrans headquarters; Sandy Elder, who graciously provided the history of the State Landmarks Department; Mr. J. Rice, who provided us with early historical data; Jim B. Gulbranson of the San Fernando Valley Archival Center; Anne D. Donahue of the Daughters of the American Revolution (DAR); Ives L. Ramos, Director General Comite de Turismo y Convenciones de Tijuana, B. C., Mexico; Melissa Phillips, AAA Research librarian; Pete and Dale Cowan; and Julia Bendímez Patterson, Instituto Nacional de Antropologia e Historia Mexicali, B.C. We also wish to thank Sunbelt Publications, Joni Harlan, and Lynne Bush for bringing this book into being.

We wish to also acknowledge the helpful and knowledgeable staffs of the following institutions:

Academy of Natural Science; Alameda Historical Society; American Automobile Association; Automobile Club of Southern California; Archdiocese of Los Angeles Archives; Bancroft Library; California Dept. of Transportation; California Historical Society; California State Automobile Club; California State Library; Campo de Cahuenga Historical Memorial Association; Historical Association of Great Britain; Historical Society of Philadelphia; University of California, Los Angeles; The Huntington Library; Institute of Historical Research, Great Britain; International Center of Photography; Kansas State Historical Society; Los Angeles Public Library; National Archives and Records Administration; New York

Historical Society; Oakland Public Library; Pennsylvania State Archives; Rhode Island Historical Society; Royal Historical Society, Great Britain; San Diego Historical Society; San Bernardino Public Library; San Francisco Public Library; San Fernando Valley Archival Center; Santa Barbara Historical Society; Southwest Museum; Sutro Library; University of California, Santa Barbara; University of California, Santa Cruz; Ventura County Foster Library; Ventura County Historical Society; Washington State Historical Society; Wichita Public Library; and Wichita State University.

THE HISTORIC CORRIDOR

A pril 27, 1996, was a beautiful, clear day in Baja California. As we stood on hard-packed ground looking around at the ancient landscape of sagebrush, cactus, and mesquite, we had a sense of how the first explorers must have felt over 300 years ago when they made their way along the Camino Real to Alta California. We had come to this historic site near the Camino Real, marking the location of the original boundary between Baja and Alta California, to witness the signing of a momentous international agreement by the three states of California: Baja California, Mexico; Baja California Sur, Mexico; and the U.S. state of California.

The faint track of El Camino Real can still be seen running across the desert floor in Baja California. (Courtesy of Harry Crosby)

While waiting for the ceremony to begin, we thought of the changes that have occurred over these many years since the Spaniards' first expedition through this area. Only the mountains remain the same. Certainly travel conditions are greatly changed. Instead of struggling with a pack train of heavily-laden mules, choking dust, scorching sun, and the severe lack of potable water, we had arrived at this historic site in air-conditioned comfort, with a plentiful supply of fresh bottled water. Instead of the din and discordance of large herds of noisy livestock, the sounds greeting us flowed from a Mexican band playing traditional music.

3

We noted another sharp contrast with the past: the presence of both Mexican and American dignitaries coming together in friendship to sign an international agreement creating an "Historic Corridor." The aim of this agreement is the mutal exploration of the natural, historical, cultural, and commercial heritage of the three states of California. From the tip of Baja California Sur to the northernmost mission at Sonoma in the state of California, this corridor of almost 2,000 miles closely follows the historic Camino Real of the Californias. Its route traverses many regions, each containing historical, natural, and cultural treasures. It was this royal road which carried the culture and language of Spanish Mexico to Alta California, thus beginning the weaving of the rich tapestry that has become the California of today. To understand how this came to be, we must explore the early history of the royal roads and how they were brought to the New World.

California's El Camino Real had its birth in sixteenth-century Spain. Although rough trails crisscrossed the country connecting small villages and rural population centers, there were no reliable roads to serve the needs of a rapidly growing commerce. The Spanish Crown felt the need for improved roads, not only to serve the population but also to expedite the transport of troops and the collection of taxes and to facilitate the transport of goods. So began a road-building program that would continue for centuries in Spain and its colonies. The focus of this early program was to create and maintain good, dependable all-weather roads leading to the city where the king was in residence. This most often was Madrid, which in time would become the capital of Spain.

The Caminos Reales were designed to be, unmistakably, roads leading to the capital city. They grew to be broad, well-maintained, beautiful highways that were protected by the military. These roads were easily identified as roads leading to the king, thus their name "Royal Road" or Camino Real. In time, business and population centers sprang up along these highways, as the Caminos Reales of Spain became the envy of all Europe.

The Spanish conquests carried the same road-building programs across the Atlantic Ocean to the New World. Throughout the Americas, wherever the Spanish flag was planted, networks of roads followed. Viceroys were appointed to rule these distant colonies in the name of the King, so

A trace of El Camino Real in present-day Baja California.

that the roads leading to the Viceroy in Mexico City were considered to be Caminos Reales. From central Mexico, these roads reached up into the American Southwest and even as far east as present-day Louisiana, serving presidios, missions, settlements, mining operations, and seaports. From mainland Mexico, they then crossed the Sea of Cortez to guide the footsteps of history up a thousand-mile-long peninsula into a beautiful new land, Alta California.

Over three hundred years ago a small group of Spaniards, Jesuit priests and soldiers, crossed the Sea of Cortez. Their goal was to establish a mission settlement on the "island" of California. With a great deal of difficulty and hardship the Jesuit order established the first permanent mission in the Californias at Nuestra Señora de Loreto Conchó, near the sapphire waters of the Sea of Cortez. During the next seven decades, this courageous group succeeded in establishing six-teen more missions in the harsh environment of what we know today as Baja California Sur, Mexico.

This land remains today largely as it was three centuries ago—an arid, harsh, incredibly hostile environment with near-ly impassable mountain ranges, scarred with deep arroyos and strewn with immense boulders. In the vast stretches of inland desert the temperatures soar to incredibly high readings during the dry months, but when the rains come, the raging waters sweep away all in their path, and new growth miraculously appears overnight. Great forests of cordón cacti crowd together so closely that neither man nor beast can pass without hacking out a path. They put one in mind of a great standing army, sometimes reaching to the very waters of the beautiful Sea of Cortez. Life in this environment was extremely difficult for conquerors and vanquished alike. Add to this the sudden, frenzied storms that would burst without warning upon the small sailing vessels bringing supplies to the peninsula, and it becomes hard to imagine how the conquest of such an uninviting land with only the most primitive of tools could have succeeded. Succeed it did, and as the missions were founded, the royal road was extended from one to the next until the expulsion of the Jesuit order from the peninsula in 1768 marked a new mandate for the use of El Camino Real.

As first the Franciscan and then the Dominican orders replaced the Jesuits on the peninsula, the door was opened for northward Spanish conquest. The goal of the expansion northward was to protect the Crown's territory from those who came in search of fur seals and whales in the coastal waters of northern California. The success of the Spanish effort was mixed. On the one hand, the "foreign influence" was never able to establish a firm foothold in the territory and, of course, more Spanish missions were established, converting many of the local inhabitants to Catholicism. Settlements grew: Farms and cattle ranches thrived in the fertile valleys. On the other hand, with the onset of political upheaval in Spain and in New Spain, the missions of Spanish California were consistently underfunded and poorly provisioned by troubled administrative centers located far to the southeast in central Mexico. The growth of the missions slowed, and with the Mexican wars of independence they declined and finally fell into disuse.

One tangible result of Spanish exploration and mission-building in Baja and Alta California, however, was the establishment of the corridor of transportation known to this day as El Camino Real. The use of the term "corridor" is deliberate here in referring to El Camino Real. It was never a fixed line on the ground, and its precise plotting shifted throughout time to accommodate changes brought about by settlement and nature's dictates.

Nuestra Señora de Loreto Conchó, Baja California Sur (circa 1900), the start of El Camino Real.

With the establishment of present-day California's first mission in San Diego in 1769, the character of El Camino Real was altered. While the road's earliest function had been to connect the Baja California missions as they were founded, now the purpose changed. It was ordered that a route be found immediately reaching far to the north of San Diego to Monterey. Here the second Spanish effort in California was the building of a presidio, or fort, on Monterey Bay. The first priority of the Spaniards was defense of their northernmost territories. Once that was accomplished, new missions were established along the already existing route. These missions served as supply outposts in support of the military presence in Monterey. Of course, the Franciscan friars were primarily concerned with the conversion of the natives, bringing a rich harvest of souls into the fold of the church. This was necessary if the indigenous peoples were to be pacified, and so the Franciscans paved the way for easy conquest by the military. Missions were established, natives instructed in Christianity, and settlements founded, but the Camino Real's primary function in that era was to support the presidios to the north.

Mission San Fernando de Velicatá, Baja California (circa 1900).

❥ The March to Alta California ❧

With a mandate from the king in hand, Captains Fernando de Rivera y Moncada and Gaspar de Portolá and a large detachment of troops, accompanied by herds of livestock, horses, and a mule train packed with supplies and trading items, traveled northward from Loreto on the Camino Real of Baja California. Their journey took them from mission to mission, over rough and often perilous trails, through narrow mountain passes, down steep arroyos, and across baking deserts. Travel over El Camino Real on the valley floors was a welcome relief. The road, which had been built by the Jesuits decades earlier, was broad and straight, and lined on either side with large rocks. Weeks after leaving Loreto, the party arrived at the northernmost site in Baja California, a staging area that would soon become San Fernando de Velicatá, the only mission on the peninsula founded by the Franciscans. Some weeks later, on his historic northward trek, Fray Junípero Serra founded this mission, his first, in 1769.

After a short rest, the party pushed on into Alta California. The 1769 route blazed by the captains from Velicatá to San Diego would become an important link in El Camino Real, connecting Alta California to the Viceroy in Mexico City.

From Loreto to Velicatá the road had linked the missions as they were established, but from San Diego north, missions would be developed along an already established Camino Real. From 1769 until after California's statehood in 1850, this road remained the main artery, first for the development of missions and then settlements in Alta California.

EL CAMINO REAL IN ALTA CALIFORNIA

Mission San Diego de Alcalá, Alta California (circa 1900).

෴

After the founding of San Diego de Alcalá, the first mission of Alta California, in 1769, the Spaniards wasted no time in commencing their next undertaking, the exploration of a land route north to Monterey, which would become the site of a presidio, a fort to signal foreign ships that Spain was ready to defend its territory.

The first journeys from San Diego to Monterey were documented in at least three diaries. The translation of Fray Juan Crespi's diary shows a carefully recorded day-by-day outline. However, matching up descriptions of the landscape with latitudes (which could be off by as much as a quarter of a mile) is very difficult, making positive identification of some sites almost impossible. The route of Portolá's first trip of exploration to locate Monterey Bay cannot be considered a "Royal Road." He did, however, blaze the trail that would become the road used at a later date to supply the settlement at Monterey. Portolá's second try was successful in establishing a route between San Diego and Monterey, thus establishing Alta California's first road, El Camino Real.

In one sense, El Camino Real in Alta California can be considered a military road. The Spanish Crown, anxious about reports of foreign ships in the eastern Pacific Ocean, and fearing encroachment into what it considered its territory, made the conquest of the lands north of the Jesuit missions their highest priority in the Californias. Although far to the north, Monterey was destined to become the first capital of Alta California. During the first few weeks of Spanish occupation of this northern point, a presidio was built and the work of converting the area's natives was begun. Later, missions would be founded along the road to support the Crown's activities in Monterey.

Travelers on this first trail were faced with an exceedingly arduous trek during even the best of seasons. From the time of Portolá's exploration on, the route of El Camino Real in Alta California varied depending on modes of travel and forces of nature. Little is known of when or where the road(s) changed. As the missions were founded, side extensions were created to service them, but the main route was always kept operational, as it was the shortest distance between San Diego, Monterey, and later, other missions to the north. The direct route from San Diego to Monterey was always maintained and used for military travel and communications, often bypassing many of the established missions in between.

Old land grant maps have been preserved in a great number of California counties. By using these, one can recover portions of the historic route. The old maps and sketches of land grants trace north-south trails, but these were not always named Camino Real. The drawings that the missionaries made are very rare. Roads (trails) were not an important part of the mission's endeavors, so they were seldom included in mission records. Only after the secularization of the missions did the land grants begin to record the names of trails and roads. They bore such names as North Road, Mission Road, Ocean Road, Camino, and a variety of others. Regardless of the name, a connection can be made back to the original Camino Real.

❧ The Branches of El Camino Real ❧

As new missions were founded El Camino Real branched out to include them. Monsignor Francis J. Weber lists five *asistencias* (small branch missions), twelve *estancias* (mission ranches), two quasi-missions (two little-known missionary efforts that were built between San Diego and Yuma, Arizona, in the western desert.[1] Little information on these survives) plus the presidios, pueblos, and the twenty-one missions. All had trails or roads connecting them to the Camino Real.

These spur routes often had separate names pertaining to the missions they serviced. The first branch of the Camino Real was to the second mission, San Carlos Borromeo de Carmelo (1770), located a few miles south of the presidio at Monterey. Although it did not claim a Camino Real name, it was used constantly by Fray Serra, early explorers, and visitors to Alta California's first capital.

Mission San José de Guadalupe, Alta California (circa 1830).

1. Msgr. Francis J. Weber, *El Caminito Real* (1988), xv.

Mission San Fernando Rey de España, Alta California (circa 1830).

With the founding of the fourth mission, San Gabriel Arcángel (1771), an addition to El Camino Real was made 121 miles north of San Diego. This new section was named El Camino Real de San Gabriel. The seventeenth mission, San Fernando Reya de España (1797), was founded 20 miles north of San Gabriel and approximately 140 miles north of San Diego. Its access road connected to the main Camino Real and was called Camino Real de San Fernando (San Fernando Mission Road). This system of naming is applied to the others as well; for example, a new branch road was made approximately 70 miles northeast of Carmelo to the fourteenth mission, San José (1797), thus creating El Camino Real de San Jose. Then, between 1817 and 1823, the Camino Real was developed to connect Mission San Rafael Arcángel and the mission at Sonoma, San Francisco Solano. This road was designated Camino Real de Sonoma. The road to Estancia San Bernardino was called Camino Real de San Bernardino. This is the only *estancia* to have a Camino Real designation.

Over the years the Franciscan friars established their missions, and roads were built to accommodate them. The missions were the only respite a weary traveler could find in

El Camino Real San Bernadino.

those days and served as rest stops on El Camino Real. In the early days of the missions there were no inns or restaurants. Often travelers were forced to sleep outside on the ground in spite of the danger from bears and, in later years, wild cattle. Of course the farther a traveler went, the greater the hardships they encountered. This is especially true for those traveling to the northernmost missions.

❧ Routes North ❦

There are two little-known routes that seem to have been sadly neglected by historians. The first is the water route to the northern missions at Sonoma and San Rafael. The second is the land route north, which we will discuss shortly.

It is generally believed that those wishing to journey to the northern missions carried their supplies to the waterfront, somewhere between the vicinity of today's Golden Gate Bridge and Fisherman's Wharf, where they boarded a boat.

*El Camino Real to
Mission San Rafael
Arcángel.*

After sailing across the channel to some location on the far side, their journey continued overland.

Some accounts written at the time give us a sense of how it was to travel across the bay. In November 1794

> . . . four natives were sent across [to San Francisco East Bay] to work with the pagans. But one of the two tule-rafts composing this armada was swept out and wrecked on the Farallones [island rocks], where two of the navigators were drowned.[2]

The historian Zephyrin Englehardt tells of a small party leaving the beach at the presidio on May 13, 1817:

> . . . taking two launches they moved across the bay to the Isla de los Angeles. They continued on the same day passing through Carquinez Strait until they reached the junction of the Sacramento River.[3]

2. Hubert H. Bancroft, *History of California, Volume 1, 1542–1800* (Santa Barbara, Calif.: Wallace Hebberd, 1963), 551.

3. Zephyrin Englehardt, *Missions and Missionaries of California, Volume 3* (1931), 27.

Harry D. Hubbard tells of a water route taken by an expedition which was sent to explore a site for the final mission, Sonoma, in June of 1823:

> A small party had gone from San Francisco, on a barge, to the mouth of Sonoma Creek. From there the party set out to explore the country about Suisun and the Napa and Sonoma Valleys.[4]

Finally, San Francisco resident George McKinstry wrote in his diary of a trip across the bay in 1847 aboard the first steamboat in California:

> On a nice bright day we left at high-tide for Sacramento with a full complement of passengers aboard. This proved to be a cranky pygmy of a craft and rolled badly every minute. It was the most uncomfortable journey I have ever made. We left San Francisco on November 28 and arrived at New Helvetia [Sacramento] December 4—six days and seven hours later.[5]

Although some historians tend to support the theory that all travelers journeying to the two northern missions went by the water route, we must question this theory. Piers and wharves were practically unknown in Alta California during the mission period. The loading and unloading of passengers and goods (which sometimes included livestock) was done by raft or barge, which carried cargo and passengers to and from shore. Sometimes cargo was simply floated to shore and live-stock were forced to swim. Thus boats, and sometimes ships, were sailed in as close to the shore as possible during high tide. As the tide receded, the craft was left anchored in the mud. Since loading could not be accomplished in the mud at low tide, it was done when the waters rose. Under such conditions, vessels could only sail at high tide.

There were other factors dictating when a vessel could sail. Periods of heavy fog were not uncommon on the bay, and because communication with the northern missions was impossible, the missionaries had no way of knowing of the impending arrival of a boat. Consequently, they would not know when to light a signal fire to guide the travelers to safe haven on the shore. For this reason night crossings

4. Harry D. Hubbard, *Vallejo* (1941), 38.
5. R. D. Hunt, *California Firsts* (Fearon Publishers, 1957), 43.

would have been highly unlikely. Therefore, the crossings were only possible during daylight hours, in clear weather, and at high tide. The extremely strong winds and treacherous currents in the bay mandated that only the most highly skilled and experienced personnel could attempt the crossing. The availability of a competent helmsman also helped determine when a ship could safely venture across the bay. Thus, crossing the bay in mission times presented somewhat erratic and possibly dangerous method of travel to the two most northern missions.

The land route, which would become El Camino Real leading to the two northernmost missions, was explored by Governor Pedro Fages and Fray Crespi in 1772. It was also used by Juan Bautista de Anza in 1774, years later by the Mexican occupation forces, and, finally, by land grant holders up to the time of the California state road system. Mission San Jose (1779) claimed all the land up through Fremont and Oakland to San Pablo and inland as far as Stockton. The increased use of the main trails in this area led to the development shortly after 1817 of a Camino Real following the coastline and connecting established ports of call. This route was one of the longest branches of El Camino Real. It was used on a continuing basis as a supply line for the two northern missions, as a passage of countless numbers of troops, and later, in the 1800s, as a supply route for development of the established of ports of call.

El Camino Real from San Jose Mission passed through Oakland, then split. One branch led to San Pablo and across the strait to San Rafael, while the other ran to Martinez, across to Benicia, and northward. This road is not well defined in California history, probably due to the fact that no missions were developed in this area. Also, with the coming of steam power, crossing the bay by water became routine and the old road fell, for the most part, into disuse. However, during the mission days it was definitely a well-traveled way. The *Grizzly Bear*, a California magazine of the time, gives us some insight into the road between the northern missions.

> At one time a splendid military road, that had been constructed by General Vallejo, traversed the greater portion of Sonoma county and much of the old road is being reincorporated in El Camino Real as it leads from the

Mission Solano de Sonoma to the old site of San Rafael, or the Hospital Mission as it was called.[6]

There is ample documentation to show that the route through Santa Clara, Alameda, Contra Costa, Solano, Napa, and Marin counties was an established branch of El Camino Real.

ฌ Alternate Routes of El Camino Real ଔ

Routes changed from time to time depending on the seasons and effects of nature, such as rainfall, earthquakes, slides, and other disasters. When the missions were moved, as many were, El Camino Real was rerouted, extended, or shortened as required to service the new mission area. A well-documented example of alternate routes of El Camino Real was to be found in Ventura County when traveling along the Rincon, the section of the route that ran along the shore between Ventura and Santa Barbara. During the dry season and at low tide, the route used was along the beach. With ebb tide the rocks were clearly visible, making travel relatively safe and dry. If the incoming tide was not too high, a person could safely walk or ride on horseback through the surf near the rocks. However, a very high tide presented obvious dangers. If the traveler had some extra time he could travel east up the canyon to Casitas, but during the rainy season this high route became a quagmire for any traveler. Thus, when the rains and high tides coincided, the already weary traveler was forced to extend his stay at the mission in Ventura or Santa Barbara, depending on his destination. These unpaved routes were used well into the early 1900s.

6. *Grizzly Bear,* June 1908, p. 36.

THE

ROAD

ॐ

If any road since the initial settlement of California could be called "California's Main Street," it would doubtless be El Camino Real. Actually, to be more precise, it was not a road at all but a trail established during the time of the missions, and used during Mexican occupation, the Gold Rush, and beyond. From the early 1800s, and as late as 1900, portions of El Camino Real could still be defined as a trail traveled by walking or riding on horseback.

By the 1840s some of the wealthy *rancheros* became the proud owners of horse-drawn carriages that allowed travel in relative comfort. This signaled the beginning of roads in California as we know them today.

Weary travelers wait for help.

The current mode of transportation was a major determinant of the route El Camino Real took. In what is now downtown Los Angeles, for instance, traders using pack trains or mules went by the mission road around the hills behind the little chapel near the present Plaza Church. When they used wagons (c. 1860), they followed the Los Angeles River around the hills near the old lime kiln, which was a well-known landmark.

With the coming of statehood in 1850 came stage-coaches, freight wagons, and various other types of wheeled carriages. The rapid increase in wheeled transportation did much to affect the development of El Camino Real, as well

Horse-drawn carriages such as this allowed travel in relative comfort. (Courtesy Ventura County Museum)

as other roads. Over the decades many things have changed in Alta California, one being the course of the roads, another being the specific (and subtle) use of the word "road." Over time, roads developed that became known as "wheeled roads." This new term pertained to roads used by carriages, wagons, and the newer vehicles, stagecoaches. Often the drivers and passengers of these new, wheeled vehicles had to endure some unpleasant conditions. In the summer, wheels and hooves ground the dirt surfaces into silt, creating choking clouds of dust. In the winter and in wet weather, mud and slush enveloped the wheels up to their hubs and axles.

ಔಞ

EL CAMINO REAL
IN TRANSITION

Travelers on the Casitas Pass Road, Ventura County. (Courtesy Ventura County Museum)

ಔಞ

D uring the 1870s and 1880s California counties became involved in the improvement of roads. An early and excellent example of San Luis Obispo County involvement was Cuesta Grade, completed in 1876. In order for El Camino Real to make the transfer from the coastal plain at San Luis Obispo to the southern end of the Salinas Valley it was necessary to cross the barrier of the Coast Range.

25

From the time of Portolá's trek this was done on a route closely following the canyon of San Luis Obispo Creek and crossing the gap at the crest of the range to the high valley on the northern side. When the final ascent was reached, it sometimes required the use of six horse teams to haul wagons and stages up the twenty-percent grade to the summit. The new, gentler path of El Camino Real was built on a twelve-percent grade and was adequate for the traffic of the time.

❧ The Stage Era ☙

Beginning in 1858 the famous Butterfield stages, carrying passengers and mail between St. Louis and San Francisco, used a portion of California's El Camino Real. After leaving the San Joaquin Valley and crossing Pacheco Pass, the stage route intersected El Camino Real at Gilroy and followed the historic old road to San Jose, finally terminating in San Francisco. Other sections of El Camino Real were used by stagecoaches, wagons, and buggies traveling from San Francisco, via San Jose, to the Oakland and Sacramento areas,

A typical overland stage.

as well as southward to Los Angeles and San Diego. Later the Butterfield line was taken over by Wells, Fargo and Company and, shortly thereafter, travel by stage was made obsolete by the coming of the transcontinental railroad.

Those early coach trips on El Camino Real were difficult at best. Frequently, in wet weather, a horseman with a shovel accompanied the coach to clean mud from the wheels. Often the main road was too narrow to allow a six-horse stage to pass a covered wagon. El Camino Real above San Buenaventura was literally a sore spot. The *Santa Barbara Press* published the report of Josephine Clifford, a stagecoach passenger, on August 3, 1886: "the rest of the night was passed inside the stage, though of sleep there was no thought, such jolting and jumping over rocks and boulders; I ache all over." Many stories are related about the trip from Santa Barbara to Ventura along the Rincon telling of the unusual ride in the water. Passengers were surprised by the sound of water rushing immediately under the coach. When they looked out, they saw the horses drawing the coach through foaming, flashing waves.

ᴕ From Trail to Road ◌ᴙ

As the population grew and trade increased, the need for better wagon roads was sharply felt, especially on El Camino Real. Rutted or muddy roads, which necessitated the use of additional teams to haul the wagons, cost farmers and merchants money and time. By the 1860s private turnpike companies were formed in some localities, El Camino Real being no exception. An example was the Alameda Turnpike Company, which maintained the road and charged tolls on the route between San Jose and Santa Clara. For a price, horsemen or teamsters could utilize an improved road. However, most commonly, the word *turnpike* referred to a company or to landowners who held a monopoly over a given route, extracted a fee, and pocketed it as almost pure profit.

Although by 1908 most of California's main wheeled roads or wagon roads were firmly established, El Camino Real was having trouble developing into a usable road. It would soon be called upon to serve another emerging form of travel, the automobile. The automobile also had its share of development problems. The combination made a drive on other than city streets a trail-breaking adventure. C. D. Cox relates his motoring expedition on El Camino Real from Nordhoff to San Luis Obispo in an unpublished document dated 1906:

> April 14. Nordhoff to Santa Barbara: crossed nine fords on the creek road and three streams in Ventura. Stuck in third. Young man with a team pulled us out. Left the road and ran through fields down a very steep hill, back on the main road. Oiled road horribly rough.

> April 24. Waited at Santa Barbara eight days for new tires from Denver. Put on new tires and went for ride. Water pump gave out. Battery repair was also necessary.

> April 25. Santa Barbara to Los Olivos: Had to stop at creek and fill radiator. Pipe working loose on top of cylinders. Road from here to Gaviota horrible. Crossed 45 creeks and canyons up one steep hill after another. Most discouraging. At Las Cruces passed automobile with broken spring. After passing Santa Ynez Mission engine missing. Took out battery and put in dry cells. Filled radiator with tumbler from horse draught.

> April 26. Los Olivos to San Luis Obispo: High wind blowing. Stopped every few minutes to tighten up water pipe, or fuss with wiring. Sand deep. More battery trouble. Broke front spring clear in two.

> April 27. San Luis Obispo: I decided to abandon car here.[7]

The kind assistance of the young man pulling Cox out of the stream did, indeed, seem to be the work of a Good Samaritan, but this was not always the case. A California State Automobile Club report tells of ranchers and farmers known to set up obstacles in order to extract towage tribute from "them rich city automobilists."

By 1890 nearly all of the private toll road franchises had been bought out by the various counties and declared to be free roads. However, their condition did not improve. Road maintenance in the period prior to state involvement was haphazard, when done at all. Engineers were scarce and counties could not afford to pay premium wages. Unqualified people were often in charge, resulting in disorganized and wasteful expenditures of public funds and substandard work.

---

7. From an unpublished manuscript by C. D. Cox, dated 1906, in the collection of the authors.

When all else failed, good old-fashioned horse power took over. (Courtesy California State Automobile Association)

Between 1867 and 1919 more than a dozen California counties issued bonds to finance the improvement of public roads, including El Camino Real. Other methods of funding included direct tax and the "pay as you go" plan. Some roads were financed by private funds and a few developed, once again, into toll roads. These methods of road reform were short lived, for lack of continued support. As the twentieth

Early state survey party on El Camino Real. (Courtesy Ventura County Museum)

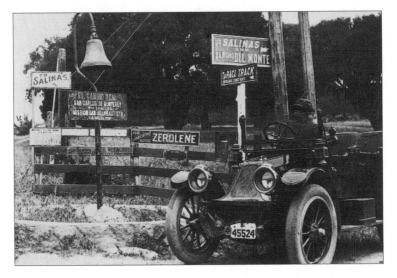

An early Auto Club road repair truck on El Camino Real. Note the reflective lettering on the bell's sign, part of efforts to make the road safer for drivers. (Courtesy Automobile Club of Southern California)

century approached, many stretches of El Camino Real were as primitive as they had been a half century earlier.

The year 1900 saw the dawn of a new century. It also saw the founding of the California State Automobile Association and the Automobile Club of Southern California. One of the most basic aspects of the clubs' drive for good roads was a volunteer program called Road Building Days. Motorland publication no. 80 (1959) reports, "Club members would converge on a stretch of road in particular need of repair and using shovels, gravel carts, split log drags, and plenty of sweat, would render it more suitable for automobile travel." Among their services in the early years the automobile clubs of California provided guidance to the state's motorists, repaired roads and bridges, and installed the first road signs.

The automobile clubs have continually shown their commitment to serving the California motorist by responding in time of emergencies and, in one instance, by keeping El Camino Real open. When the Santa Margarita River flooded in San Diego County, the Automobile Club of Southern California built a temporary bridge, providing the only means of crossing.

The Auto Club's temporary bridge across the Santa Margarita River.
(Courtesy Automobile Club of Southern California)

By 1890 it seemed that California's roads were destined to disintegrate, but a movement came to the forefront that would affect not only El Camino Real but also the entire state of California: the "Good Roads Movement."

❧ The Good Roads Movement ❦

On March 27, 1895, Governor Henry H. Markham created the Bureau of Highways. He appointed three initial members to this bureau: R. C. Irvine of Sacramento; Marsden Manson of San Francisco; and J. C. Maude of Riverside. The creation of this bureau and its actions provided the necessary impetus for the Good Roads Movement. As a result of the activity of the Bureau of Highways, the press throughout the state began to agitate for better roads. The *Los Angeles Times* of January 18, 1896, editorialized,

> If the State were to build a few hundred miles of first class highway, the benefit would be so great and so apparent that the movement for good roads would be greatly accelerated and the people would cheerfully furnish the money necessary to continue the work until all the principal roads in the State were improved.

This expression of editorial opinion seems to indicate a widespread public interest in road improvement. In fact, this interest dated even farther back than 1895. In 1893 a good roads convention was held in the senate chamber in Sacramento under the encouragement of Governor Markham. Although a state highway system was discussed, no definite decisions resulted.

The Bureau of Highways lasted only two years, being replaced on April 1, 1897 by the Department of Highways. In 1907 the State Department of Engineering was created, and on March 22, 1909, Governor James Gillette presented a bill that would establish a California Highway Commission.

Under the first state bond issue, passed in 1910, a dual-lane system was proposed, with two main highways extending from Mexico to Oregon: one traversed the great central valleys; the other, named El Camino Real, traveled along the western slope of the Coast Range.

ഇ Adventure or Nightmare? ര

After 1909, the motorist with a good sense of adventure and lots of time, and with much effort, luck, and frustration, could find his or her way from San Francisco to Los Angeles and on to San Diego using the newly installed El Camino Real Bell road markers. Complete, detailed road maps would not be available to the motorist for another three years.

In 1912 the American Automobile Association (AAA) published its first strip maps of the San Diego to San Francisco route for the new adventure seekers they called "autoists." In the early years of the twentieth century, travel by automobile over El Camino Real was an adventure or a nightmare, depending on one's attitude and the season of the year. Directions were printed in the newspapers and popular magazines, as well as in the California State Automobile Association (CSAA) 1912 *Tour Book*. Even when available, some of the information proved to be less than helpful.

To illustrate the road conditions and routing of El Camino Real, a typical trip from San Francisco to Los Angeles is described.[8] Our traveler has a new Kissel car, and, during the spring of 1912, he and a companion begin their journey. They navigate through the streets of the recently rebuilt city of San Francisco, turning on to Mission Street, which takes them south to the county line within thirty-five minutes. They travel down a wide macadamized highway, lined with tall trees, past the cemetery at Colma. Although the road has been improved, it is full of chuckholes. The route they are traveling is not a continuous road but, rather, involves a series of turns through the cities of the peninsula. They navigate with the help of the 1912 *Tour Book*. It contains strip maps showing all bridges, intersecting roads, and the grades in steep areas. Its introduction states,

> The accurate detail of the maps and the advantages of the information reading in both directions are so obvious as to require no special comment. The maps will be found especially accurate since they were drawn from the seat of the [Kissel] Pathfinder Car, by an expert graduate Civil Engineer. Nothing has been done "by guess."

Indeed, with few signs posted and only El Camino Real Bells as guides, finding one's way to Los Angeles would have been a frustrating experience without a good map. Advertisements throughout the book were not only informative, telling the motorist what services were available and where, but they also helped defray the cost of publication. The *Tour Book* advises: "Care should be taken by association members and automobilists in general to patronize those who have patronized our publication."

---

8. The account is taken from an unpublished manuscript dated 1978, author unknown, in the collection of the authors.

Upon reaching San Jose, the navigator consults another guide, mostly for curiosity's sake. It is an article from a *Sunset* magazine of the previous year. The directions are far less detailed than the *Tour Book*:

> At San Jose continue out the main street, upon which the Vendome and St. James Hotels are located, in order to be certain that you strike the Gilroy road. In Gilroy, follow right along the main street, keeping to that road until San Juan is reached by way of Sargent's. Upon reaching mission town, run by the Plaza Hotel, opposite the Mission, and then turn at right angles for two squares, then one to the left, and the road running to your right is the one that leads to the base of the San Juan Grade.

The road over the San Juan Grade is steep, with eight- to fifteen-percent grades, but once its dust and rocks are passed it is easier driving down to the Salinas Valley. Care is taken driving through Salinas that the speed limits are not exceeded. In 1905 the state vehicle law set the speed limits at ten miles per hour in built-up areas (cities), fifteen miles per hour in towns, and twenty miles per hour in open country. It varies in different cities so that it is difficult to know the precise law for each locality. The road beyond Salinas as far as Gonzales is excellent macadam, and the Kissel is daringly brought up thirty-five miles per hour before slowing back down to the normal twenty at the suggestion of the nervous navigator. El Camino Real deteriorates south of Gonzales and the left front tire soon goes flat. Good luck has been riding with them so far, as this is their first flat. After a roadside patch job, they are on their way again. Since the car is new, the tires are still in good shape. However, they are not expected to last much beyond 3,000 miles.

It is late afternoon when they face the last barrier of the day, the Jolon Grade. The fifteen-percent winding ascent is made and, over an easier descent, the last seven miles are covered to Jolon, where they stop at Dutton's Hotel for a well-earned respite from the dust and jarring of the previous 170 miles.

Early the next morning, the travelers are back on El Camino Real heading southeast through the beautiful oak valleys toward the Salinas River at Bradley. The Salinas River is low at this time of year so the wet weather route can be avoided. That long, looping, nine-mile detour into the hills by way of Indian Valley avoids fording the Salinas River, which is impossible during high water.

Once the river is forded, the next barrier to be traversed is Cuesta Grade. The eight- to ten-percent grade of the northern approach is not severe, but the long descent on the southern slope, with grades of over twelve percent, is a true test of the brakes. The road is good, although quite serpentine, and the travelers stop at San Luis Obispo at the foot of the grade for gasoline and a brief rest. There is no gas gauge, so it is necessary to dip a stick into the tank to check the fuel level. The gas is purchased at a garage, as the first "drive-in" filling station will not open until December 1913. In some remote places it is still necessary to purchase gasoline in a general store, where it is sold in large cans.

Beyond San Luis Obispo, sharp turns and sand are encountered around Arroyo Grande. They notice a car parked just off the road adjacent to some dense bushes, and speculate that the occupants of that car are most likely "picking flowers." This is a euphemism used in the time before the advent of service stations and their restroom facilities.

South of Santa Maria, Foxen Canyon is the preferred route. The road leads over two short hills, the latter containing a very steep twenty-percent grade, testing two tired "autoists" and a tired car, before they pull into Los Olivos for their second night's lodging at Mattei's Tavern. They have traveled 144 miles today and have journeyed a total of 314 miles from San Francisco.

The next day the San Marcos Pass route is avoided because of its excessive grades of over twenty-five percent, and the auto is guided past Mission Santa Ynez toward the next barrier, Gaviota Pass. The descent is steep and cut from solid rock. The *Tour Book* mentions the many sharp turns and advises that "skillful, careful driving will be necessary."

They reach the Pacific Ocean. In many ways, the thirty miles to Santa Barbara is the most difficult stretch they will face. It is not much more than a trail winding in and out of the barrancas, which cut through the plain lying between the Santa Ynez Mountains and the ocean. It is rocky and abounds in steep pitches of up to eighteen percent. In one five-mile stretch, sharp rocks result in three flat tires. They have seen the survey stakes for the state highway in several locations along their route, particularly along this stretch.

*The unimproved (and somewhat daunting!) El Camino Real through
Gaviota Pass, north of Santa Barbara.*

At Goleta, a few miles west of Santa Barbara, the road
is much improved by the work of Santa Barbara County. The
travelers enjoy the lush greenery of beautiful Santa Barbara
and the Hope Ranch. Their joy is unbounded as they
smoothly roll along a portion of dust-free, hard-surfaced road
through Montecito. Their pleasure is short-lived, however, as
the pavement ends and they again bump their way toward
Los Angeles.

The navigator tells of an article he has recently read
about the wooden causeway being built along the coast near
Rincon Point. They both lament its unfinished condition as
they are forced inland over the double summits of Casitas
Pass, down into Ventura.

Once past Camarillo, the final major incline before Los
Angeles is the Conejo Grade. The climb is not terribly tax-
ing to the car, as the grade is less than ten percent and the
road is very good. Twenty miles of a rolling, easily-followed
road brings them to Calabasas. They get their first glimpse
of the San Fernando Valley and realize that their journey is

Bicyclists on Cahuenga Pass, circa 1899.

almost ended. Rolling over a good road through Los Angeles County, much of which is oiled (oil, being an excellent dust palliative, is much used by Los Angeles County), the travelers descend the Cahuenga Grade into Hollywood at dusk. Driving past the Los Angeles City Hall, the driver checks his odometer and determines the total distance traveled from San Francisco to be 475.5 miles. They agree that it is quite close to the 472.2 miles shown in the *Tour Guide* and heartily rejoice the successful completion of their motor tour. They are both amazed as they recall that almost six years earlier, two men in a Pope-Hartford had made the same trip in seventeen hours and fifty-five minutes. However, they agree that their driving time of just over thirty-nine hours is far more typical.

ᔓ The Transition Continues ᔕ

The State Highway Commission was charged with maintaining and properly naming the state road system. As a result of all of the early days of squabbling about potential routes, in 1910 California Highway 2 was named El Camino Real. Many years later Highway 2 was redesignated Highway 101.

With the advent of modern engineering and road-building equipment, Highway 101 developed into one of the state's best highways, traveling the entire length of the state from its national boundary with Mexico to the Oregon state line. The southern portion of it, as far north as Sonoma, was, of course, El Camino Real.

By the end of 1920, it was possible to drive the entire distance of El Camino Real on pavement with the exception of a few short gaps. In 1926 the Highway Commission was able to report the elimination of the last unpaved section of El Camino Real on Conejo Grade.

El Camino Real has seen many uses, but some citizens put it to new use. A 1950 issue of the *California Highways and Public Works* magazine tells of a report found in the 1910 *San Mateo County Press*. Reportedly, the young folk of the peninsula towns had taken up the fad of utilizing the new state highway for roller recreation. Evidently, moonlight skating parties were quite a common activity on the new smooth surface of El Camino Real.

From the turn of the century on, the "good old days"of El Camino Real faded with each passing year. With the rapid increase in population and commerce, the scenic aspects of El Camino Real were to change rapidly. A prime example was the disappearance of the beautiful tree-lined section of El Camino Real between Santa Clara and San Jose, known as the Alameda.

The mid-1930s saw the commencement of four-lane construction on many portions of El Camino Real. The year 1941 heralded the beginning of the United States' direct involvement in World War II and, by that year, all but a few miles of El Camino Real had been rebuilt—much of it completely relocated. The highway was in excellent condition and quite satisfactory for the current demands, perhaps more so than at any time in its history. Although World War II brought an end to almost all construction on El Camino Real, the end of hostilities found El Camino Real ready for the great era of freeway construction.

SAVING EL CAMINO REAL

El Camino Real bell and plaque placed in front of the home of Eileen Dismuke, Santa Barbara.

෨෩

S ince El Camino Real's beginnings in Alta California in 1767 there have been several times when it was in danger of being lost, especially in name. The first was following the occupation of California by Mexico, when the newly appointed Governor José María Echeandía of California tried to make some drastic changes. One of these was changing the name of El Camino Real to the Republican Turnpike. If it were not for a filing error in Mexico City, this historic road name might have been lost forever.

During the 1904 meeting in Los Angeles to plan for El Camino Real's preservation, a delegate attempted to scuttle the entire project with his remarks. As reported by Charles Lummis, "There was even one gentleman who assured the convention 'that there never was a Camino Real in California.'"

The most startling event, however, was the 1957 California State Legislature's blunder of the decade, the renaming of El Camino Real, a legislative blunder that sparked the rebirth of an El Camino Real lobby, this time known as the Committee for El Camino Real.

The following is a personal account by Mrs. Eileen C. Dismuke, Past Grand President, Native Daughters of the Golden West (NDGW), from her letter of April 15, 1974, to Mrs. Loretta Trathen of Grass Valley, California:

> When I made my first official journey as Grand President to Marysville, in July of 1958, to attend a 50th Anniversary of that Parlor, I found, as I traveled Highway 101 from Santa Barbara north, in Santa Barbara county, a large highway sign which announced that this was "Cabrillo Highway". My hair practically stood on end, and I remarked to my traveling companion on that trip that I was at a loss to understand the naming of our highway "Cabrillo Highway," when it had been known, since the coming of Padre Junípero Serra in 1776, as "El Camino Real."

> On my return to San Francisco from Marysville that week, for a tea at the Native Daughter Home as a benefit for our restoration of Mission Soledad, I had occasion to visit with the Rev. David Temple, O.F.M., who at that time was Provincial of the St. Barbara Province, with headquarters in Oakland, and had been invited to our Mission Soledad Tea. I told him of seeing the Cabrillo Highway signs on 101 all the way from Santa Barbara to San Francisco, and asked him if he was aware of them and their meaning. He said he had just learned of them, that he did not know the reason for their being there, but thought we should look into the matter.

A modern sign for the troublesome Cabrillo Highway.

On my return to Santa Barbara, I telephoned our State Senator, the late J. J. Hollister, to ask him for an explanation of the Cabrillo Highway signs. He explained that this was a mistake of the 1957 Legislature, that the intent had been to name Highway 1, between Las Cruces and San Francisco, which we know as the San Simeon Highway, "Cabrillo Highway," but that when the legislation was in process of being written, the wrong highway designation numbers had been given, and instead of Highway 1, from the area designated above being given, that highway numbers for Highway 101 between San Diego and San Francisco had been furnished for the legislation, and as a result our "El Camino Real" had been renamed "Cabrillo Highway."

I asked Senator Hollister what could be done to correct this mistake. He volunteered to put a bill in the hopper in January 1959, but said he would have to have a strong lobby to back him up because the state had spent about $50,000 to have the signs made and in addition there had been considerable expense in installation. He stated that the Cabrillo Clubs of California had been sponsors of the original legislation, and he was sure they would not willingly give up the legislation without a fight, so we had both the legislature and the Cabrillo Clubs to worry about in trying to reverse the 1957 legislation.

However, in January 1959 Senator Hollister introduced Senate Bill No. 123 providing for return of the name "El Camino Real" to the highway from San Diego to San Francisco via Highway 101. I had occasion to make trips to Sacramento a number of times that spring on behalf of this bill, appearing before the Transportation, Finance, and Ways and Means Committees, and I learned that all of our legislators in the Assembly and Senate had been bombarded with letters from our Parlors and individual members asking support of this legislation, as a result of my bulletins as Grand President. The Bill had successfully gotten through all of the Assembly and Senate Committees to which it was referred, and had passed the Assembly. The last hurdle was the Senate Hearing, and, on April 19, at about 9:00 a.m. I received a telephone call from Irma Murray, our Grand Secretary, telling me that the Executive Secretary for the Committee for El Camino Real, Ralph Buffon, had just phoned her to ask that she relay a message to me of the urgency of my getting over to Sacramento that morning. The Senator from Kings County had objected to passage of the bill at the hearing the day before, and unless I could convince him to withdraw his objection, the bill would die in the Senate. I hurriedly jumped in my car and got over to Sacramento, where Senator Hollister gave me a card of introduction to the Senator from Kings County, and I went to his office. It was 3:00 p.m. again that afternoon. I had to wait for another interview to end before getting in to the Senator from Kings County. When I did, I told him of my anxiety about this Bill, that since it was a mistake of the 1957 legislature I felt that it should be changed, and that there were many more Native Sons and Native Daughters of the Golden West in California than there were Cabrillo Club members who wanted this legislation reversed. He asked me where the Native Sons and Native Daughters were in 1957 when this legislation was being considered. I told him that was a good question, but I didn't have an answer—that the first I learned of it was when I saw the "Cabrillo Highway" sign on 101, and learned from Senator Hollister the reason therefore. He told me he had had a call from Father David Temple that morning asking him to reconsider this vote, and then he smiled and told me that when he went back into session that afternoon he would withdraw his objection. I was overjoyed, as you can imagine. I rushed back up to Senator Hollister's office to get a pass into the Senate, and waited for S.B. 123 to be called up again. I was due in Paradise at 6:30 p.m. for a dinner and official visit that night, but could not leave Sacramento until I knew the bill has successfully passed the Senate. Two other bills were called up first, and finally, S.B. 123 was called by the speaker of the Senate. Immediately the Senator from Kings County stood (he was a handsome man, tall and broad shouldered, with a beautiful shock of white, wavy hair), and he withdrew his objection. In the next instant, Senator Hollister was on his feet to move for approval of the bill. And it was passed unanimously. I then practically flew to Paradise in my little Plymouth, arriving almost an hour late, but the Parlor understood the reason for my delay.

Now, during the deliberations on S.B. 123, I learned that then Assemblyman Jack Shrade, from San Diego, (who is now a Senator from San Diego), had put a Bill in the 1957 Legislature asking for return of El Camino Real Bells at accesses to Old Mission Communities, such as San Diego, San Juan Capistrano, Ventura, Santa Barbara, etc. His bill had not gotten through the 1957 legislative year, and he brought it back for consideration in the 1959 legislature. When we learned this, our Committee for El Camino Real, which had been formulated at my call in December 1958 to back Senator Hollister and his S.B. 123 for return of the name to the highway, assisted Assemblyman Schrade with his legislation for return of the bells to the highway, and the impetus of our legislation returning the name to the highway was responsible in large part for the passage of the bell legislation.

In 1986 a bell was placed in front of the Santa Barbara home of Eileen Dismuke. A bronze plaque at the base of the bell reads:

> In Memory of Eileen Galvin Dismuke
> Past Grand President
> Whose Love for Her State
> And El Camino Real Project
> Will Never Be Forgotten

So A Little White Line &#x08;

In 1902 The California Federation of Women's Clubs (CFWC) endorsed the project of saving El Camino Real of California. Over the years these dedicated women participated in marking El Camino Real as a historic road, as well as setting safety standards for all California roads (indeed, for the highways of the nation as well). The following account is adapted from the CFWC book *A Bouquet of Memories*. It is the history of a little white line and of its originator, Dr. June A. W. McCarroll, a pioneer physician of Coachella Valley.

> In the fall of 1917, I became the proud possessor of a Model-T Ford, and being accustomed to an out-of-door life, I tried going everywhere with my new car. It gave a person a free feeling, until I met a truck on the paved highway between Indio and Edom. Those who have driven on the old-time fifteen-foot pavement with no shoulders but eight to ten inches of very soft sand, and met a truck loaded eight to ten feet wide, keeping well over the middle, can realize what happened to me. Believing that something should be done, I began talking about a central road line to nearly anyone who would listen to me. The Escondido Chamber of Commerce was one of the first to pass a resolution supporting the movement, followed by various organizations, but none took real action toward development. In 1918 George Bigalow was interested in an Ocean-to-Ocean Highway routed through Coachella Valley. He made it possible for my affidavit to be sent to the County Chamber of Commerce of Fresno during 1934 when that body conducted a search for the author of the middle highway line for the Goodrich Tire Company.

> It was presented to the Riverside Board of Supervisors, in 1918, by board member Mr. Charles Hamilton of Banning. They endorsed it but had no money to spend on roads.

> When Mr. Darlington was chairman of the State Highway Commission, the matter of a line down the middle of the highway was presented to him, but owing to the expense involved, he felt traffic was not sufficiently heavy to warrant the project.

> When Mrs. Ada DeNyse became Riverside County president in 1923, she appointed me chairman of Good Roads.

About that time I also came to the conclusion that talking to men's organizations accomplished little. After five years of persistent effort I seemed to be getting nowhere. Up to this point my club activities had been along the so-called "women's lines." However, still obsessed with the "white line" idea and realizing I had accomplished nothing with men's organizations, I decided I would work with the women.

During this time, an eight-mile stretch of paved road eight feet wide, from Kane Spring to Westmorland, was doubled in width. The truck drivers told me that on that stretch of highway, with the edge of the former surface showing so plainly, they could readily tell where the center was, which they found a great help. All of this I embodied into a reso-lution petitioning the state legislature to enact a law authorizing the State Highway Commission to paint a line in the middle of all state roads. My own club, the Women's Club of Indio, unanimously endorsed this resolution, which soon started merrily on its way. I then carried this resolution through the County, the District, and the State Federation of Women's Clubs, with their full sanction and support. Now, with the force of the federation behind it, my pet project began to assume real proportion.

Copies of this resolution, with endorsements, were given to our Riverside Assemblyman A. C. Murrey, who prepared a bill for the legislature. Also interested was Harvey C. Troy, State Highway Commission chair. Money had been raised to send me to Sacramento to work for the passage of the bill.

In November 1924, Assemblyman Murrey came to speak before the Indio Women's Club on amendments and saying the State Highway Commission chairman had agreed to try my idea.

When I gave this idea to a needy world, it was with no thought of honors, only safety for drivers of automobiles. The entire Federation of Women's Clubs organization has given time and strong influence to make the line a reality, and I truly thank them, and the Riverside County Federation and my own Indio Women's Club which stood by through all the hard uphill years.[9]

9. Adapted from California Federation of Women's Clubs, *A Bouquet of Memories* (Fresno, Calif.: Monica's Printing Arts, 1991).

After nearly a century of waiting for proper recognition, the California Federation of Women's Clubs was finally rewarded when Caltrans, on November 22, 1999, acknowledged that they were the originators of the first state-wide road safety concept in the history of California highways, a little white line.

The State Historical Landmarks Commission

Official recognition of California historical sites began in Los Angeles in 1895 with the formation of the Landmarks Club, which was dedicated to the preservation of historical sites starting with the Spanish missions. In 1902, the California Historical Landmarks League was incorporated in San Francisco for similar purposes.

The landmark program became official in 1931, when legislation required the director of the Department of Natural Resources "to register and mark buildings of historical interest or landmarks." The Natural Resources Director delegated the California State Chamber of Commerce to administer the program. The committee formed to evaluate potential sites included some of the most prestigious historians of the time: Abrey Drury; Francis Farquhar; Carl I. Wheat, Herbert Bolton; DeWitt V. Hutchings; Senator Leroy A. White; and Lawrence Hill.

The first twenty landmarks were officially designated on June 1, 1932. The emphasis was on well-known places and events in California history, especially missions, early settlements, battlegrounds, and Gold Rush sites. By the end of the program's first year, a total of seventy-eight historical landmarks had been registered.

Many early markers were placed through the efforts of such groups as the Native Sons of the Golden West, Native Daughters of the Golden West, and the Daughters of the American Revolution. These and other historically motivated organizations carried on a marker program until 1948, the centennial year of the discovery of gold at Sutter's Mill, when the state legislature set up the California Centennial Commission.

This early program was ambitious, but not without its quirks. Landmarks were registered without criteria, documentation requirements were minimal, and some properties were registered simply on the basis of hearsay or local legend. To assure greater integrity and credibility, Governor Earl Warren created the California Historical Landmarks Advisory Committee in May 1949. In 1962 the committee adopted registration criteria. Strict adherence to these criteria has lent dignity and integrity to the landmark program.

Legislation in 1974 changed the California Historical Landmarks Advisory Committee to the State Historical Resources Commission. The commission has adopted a policy for marking satellite or thematic landmarks that are related to an existing California Registered Historical Landmark. Satellite landmarks are related sites that have the same number as the first application, but with the addition of a hyphen and the number "1," "2," and so on. A few landmarks are related to one another by a theme (thematic landmark) that identifies their historical, social, or architectural significance, but are not sites integrally identified with, or contiguous with one another. Examples include Native-American ceremonial roundhouses (No. 100), Century folk-art environments (No. 939), Light stations of California (No. 951), Japanese-American temporary detention camps (No. 934) and El Camino Real (No. 784).

In 1962 Father Noel Moholy, O.F.M., was appointed to the California Historical Landmarks Advisory Committee. He attended his first meeting on July 27, 1962, in Cambria, San Luis Obispo County. At the October 19, 1962 meeting Father Moholy presented the suggestion to place plaques at the northern and southern end of "El Camino Real As Father Serra Knew It." He indicated he would see that a formal application was presented to the committee at its next meeting.

At the January 8, 1963, meeting of the California Historical Landmarks Advisory Committee, a formal application for the designation of "El Camino Real (As Father Serra Knew It and Helped Blaze It), from San Diego County to, and including, San Francisco County" was presented and approved. As part of the plaque allocation approval, the committee indicated that, besides an official landmark plaque for the north and south, each county along El Camino Real

Plaque placed by the state of California near the northern end of El Camino Real in commemoration of Father Serra's 250th birthday.

would be entitled to one plaque to be placed on the most significant site within its boundaries.

To commemorate the 250th anniversary of Father Serra's birth, plans were made to dedicate two plaques in 1963. The northern plaque, located at Mission San Francisco de Asís, was dedicated November 21, 1963, and the southern plaque, for San Diego County, located at Mission San Diego de Alcalá, was dedicated December 19, 1963.

THE

BELLS

W hen, in the seventeenth century, El Camino Real was extended northward into Nueva California, the road was under the dominion of men. Men explored the territory and decided on the routes. Men cleared the trail and men walked or rode upon it, driving livestock or leading pack trains. Soldiers, male neophytes, and clergy were the first to work on and make use of the new passage to the north. Later, when colonists were sent to settle in the new land, women made an appearance, but dominion over and

Native Daughters of the Golden West, San Luisita Parlor No. 108, September 10, 1908.

control of all things pertaining to the new road rested with men. At this point in time, El Camino Real was a tool, a most important tool to be sure, but nevertheless, it was solely a means to an end. It seems doubtful that most people, in that time and place, ever gave it a second thought.

Early in the twentieth century this attitude suddenly changed. This ancient road was no longer merely a half-forgotten passageway from point to point. El Camino Real became an important symbol of early California. It was now

51

a rapidly vanishing part of history. Those who stepped forward to rally support for preserving El Camino Real of California were women. From that point on, the women of California were the dominant force concerning the oldest roadway in the state.

The story that follows is one of remarkable dedication and tireless effort in the crusade to identify, preserve, and symbolically mark El Camino Real of California. It is the astounding story of women united, over the course of a century, in a common cause, a cause that continues today with ever renewed vitality. All Californians, present and future, owe an immense debt of gratitude to these amazing women and to the organizations within which they work.

THE BIRTH OF AN IDEA

First bell placed at Loreto, Baja California Sur.

ঙ৩ঙ৩

The first recorded mention of a plan to save El Camino Real of California came from Anna Pitcher (alternately spelled Picher) of Pasadena in 1892. Miss Pitcher, then director of the Pasadena Art Exhibition Association, was active in social clubs and the Southwest Museum. Mrs. A. S. C. Forbes informs us that

> Miss Pitcher was also active in fund raising for the fledgling Pasadena Public Library (1889) and arranged a thirteen-volume display of articles from leading western maga-

53

zines that was shown at the Paris International Exposition, and at the National Education convention in Los Angeles, before coming home.[10]

According to Gertrude Stoughton,

> Miss Pitcher suggested and maintained the idea that the California Franciscan Missions as "stations" on the Camino Real were the most important art treasure in the possession of the State of California.[11]

From 1892 till 1902 Anna Pitcher contacted many organizations to generate interest in a project to preserve El Camino Real, but without success. She was well acquainted with Charles Lummis and his efforts to preserve the old missions, now in a state of decay, along the early route of El Camino Real. Mr. Lummis encouraged her, but his efforts were concentrated on the missions, not the road.

ஐ A Statewide Project ைஐ

In 1902 Miss Pitcher had the opportunity to present her plan to two of the most influential organizations in California at that time. The first wide publicity given to saving El Camino Real occurred when the general plan for the project was formally presented before the meeting of the Sixth Biennial of the General Federation of Women's Clubs, held in Los Angeles in May of that year. The federation, realizing that this was a worthy cause, voted to adopt Miss Pitcher's proposal and assigned it to their newly formed History and Landmarks Department, chaired by Mrs. A. S. C. Forbes.[12]

Miss Pitcher's five-point proposal for saving El Camino Real included:

1. Tracing the original Government Road of Spanish California from San Diego to San Francisco Solano

10. A. S. C. Forbes, *California Missions and Landmarks*, 8th ed., p. 354.

11. Gertrude K. Stoughton, *The Books of California* (Los Angeles, Calif.: Ward Ritchie Press, 1968), pp. 109–13.

12. Much to Mrs. Forbes' surprise, she found that Miss Pitcher was a neighbor. They both lived on Grand Avenue in Pasadena. It is not recorded, but it seems reasonable to speculate that these two ladies spent time together sharing their ideas and dreams for this project.

through present succeeding counties and recording the history and traditions of this Road.

2. Proving the present adaptability of portions of the road for the purpose of a California State Highway, with the 21 Franciscan missions as both stations and landmarks upon it, one day's journey apart.

3. Petitioning County Supervisors to assist the movement and record by County Surveyors of the present road, where it exists, and its intersection with other roads and boulevards suitable for a State Highway.

4. Further petitioning Supervisors to unite in asking the State of California to survey the existing portions of this Camino Real and put milestones upon it which shall record its history.

5. Interesting residents and strangers in gradually making this road into a MEMORIAL HIGHWAY, preserving its Spanish name, as well as making this route a model road meeting Government approval.

It should be noted that in 1902 Miss Pitcher presented only this brief outline of her plan. Details of how this program was to be implemented were still years in the future.

In June 1902 the same plan for saving El Camino Real was presented by Miss Pitcher to the Grand Parlor of the Native Daughters of the Golden West, then in session in Los Angeles. The Grand Parlor gave their endorsement but no action was taken until years later.

In late 1902, when Miss Pitcher became seriously ill, more than a decade of dedicated work was in danger of being abandoned. On December 30, 1902, she sent a letter to Mrs. Buckley, state president of the California Federation of Women's Clubs, placing the continuation of the work with this organization.

> Nothing would be quite so desirable as the presentation (at the State Convention) of the Camino Real by Mrs. Forbes. I would like the road plan taken up both as California History and Landmarks work. Let me say again how anxious I am to reach Oakland and the north for the Camino Real plan.[13]

13. Annual Report of the CFWC, 1902–1903.

Mrs. Forbes, a very resourceful person, fully understood the significance of this project. She accepted the challenge, and continued Anna Pitcher's crusade for the preservation of El Camino Real. Mrs. Forbes was in an excellent position to assume this role, as she was a member of numerous service clubs and organizations, including the Friday Morning Club, the Southern California Historical Society, Women's Press Club, and the Ruskin Art Club. She had already secured her place in California history by finding an important historical document which had been lost for many years.

Mrs. Forbes was responsible for the discovery of a lost treaty signed by Colonel John C. Frémont and General Andrés Pico which proved that Frémont, whether justified or not in exercising such authority, had secured California for the United States. Under the auspices of the Historical Society of Southern California, Mrs. Forbes helped establish the historic park Campo de Cahuenga where the treaty had been signed.[14]

₭ The Project Begins ⁒

Mrs. Forbes and Mrs. Caroline R. Olney, both members of the California Federation of Women's Clubs, outlined a plan for the establishment of a state-wide organization committed to the restoration of El Camino Real. What was needed was communication with the state legislature. Mrs. Olney, an Oakland Club member then living in Los Angeles, had contacts in Sacramento and could provide information on pending legislation concerning the state road bills movement in the California Department of Transportation and state Public Works Department. Everything seemed in place for the next phase, a meeting to include state and county officials.

Almost immediately, however, the idea of a statewide organization was met with opposition. Some CFWC members wanted it to be a federation project, since Mrs. Forbes was a CFWC member and the federation was the first to adopt the project. There were objections from certain members of the Landmarks Club, who felt this plan should be under their direction. Some members wanted to improve only that part of El Camino Real located south of the Tehachapi

14. *Southern California Quarterly*, vol. 28 (1968): 80-81.

Mountains. This faction also opposed state aid in the reconstruction of the route.

Mrs. Forbes and Mrs. Olney continued to base the project on the original plan, which included state aid and entailed the research and restoration of the entire length of the road that once connected the historic California missions from San Diego to Sonoma. The route was to be marked with some kind of symbol identifying it as El Camino Real. This project was adopted by the California Federation of Women's Clubs and the Native Daughters of the Golden West, the automobile clubs, the good roads clubs, and historical societies. They appealed to all broad-minded, future-thinking individuals for support. Their persistence was rewarded, but not without a struggle.

∞ The Los Angeles Convention ∞

During the early part of the century, the Los Angeles Chamber of Commerce (LACC) aggressively promoted the mutually beneficial causes of local business and good roads. Through the persuasion of Mr. A. S. C. Forbes, a member of the LACC, contact with the Landmarks Club, and a host of other organizations making known their desire for saving this historic road, a convention was convened on January 30, 1904, to consider Miss Pitcher's five-point plan.

Invitations to the January gathering went out to other chambers of commerce, Native Sons and Daughters groups, county supervisors, historical societies, women's clubs, automobile clubs, and many commercial organizations. It has been frequently noted that all eighty invited delegates attended.

The Los Angeles Chamber of Commerce agenda for consideration can be summarized as:

1. Constructing and marking a great thoroughfare to follow the line of the ancient El Camino Real from San Diego to Santa Barbara.

2. Asking the northern counties to cooperate and undertake the project from Santa Barbara northward.

Comments on the meeting by Charles Lummis in *Outwest* (1904) elaborate on the plan.

The great modern highway along the historic line will be for automobilists, bicyclists, and tallyhos, indeed—but it will also be for the farmers, who amount to a good deal more, for the quiet drivers, for the people that can sit on a horse without falling off, for people who still have joy of walking. It will even be for our tourists; and while we sometimes detect in them certain lapses from wisdom, few of them are such fools as to wish to snort up the pike at sixty miles an hour and never see the missions or the country.[15]

The political maneuvering and back-room politics that occurred at this Los Angeles meeting prompted a frustrated Charles Lummis to report in the same publication:

For the Convention did not consider at all the things for which it was called. The lady from Sacramento [Mrs. C. Olney] had been busy. By circulating the foolish falsehood that the Camino Real plan was a masked move for State Division, she excited the Sons and Native Daughters—two patriotic organizations which stand for "California one and indivisible," as do we all. . . . But these organizations were imposed upon by this childish story; their delegates controlled the convention; and the delegates had their instructions. It was an entirely innocent act on the part of the California-born Americans, many of whom are now raging at the knowledge of the deceit that was practiced upon them, and the position in which this place-hunter put the two orders as apparently ignorant and careless of the history of the State they love.[16]

Two resolutions were passed at the January 30 meeting. First, a committee of fifteen persons was to be appointed to make the necessary arrangements and to draft a call for a convention to organize a permanent statewide Camino Real Association. The second resolution, according to Lummis, called for a Camino Real "coterminous with the limits of the State."

The arrangements, planning, and call for a second convention were completed. This meeting was to be held April 19–20, 1904, at Santa Barbara. Delegates from each part of the state through which El Camino Real passed, including many organizations, clubs, and leading newspapers, were invited to attend.

15. Charles Lummis, *Outwest* (February 1904), p. 17.
16. Charles Lummis, *Outwest* (February 1904), p. 17.

CALL FOR STATE CONVENTION.

A State Convention is hereby called to be held at Santa Barbara, on the 19th and 20th days of April, A. D. 1904, for the organization of a State Camino Real Association, and the election of delegates to the National Good Roads Convention, to be held at St. Louis, on May 16th to 21st inclusive, 1904. Convention to convene at two o'clock P. M. of April 19th.

The object and purpose of the Association to be formed is to be nearly as possible as follows:

First. To unite all the commercial, social and agricultural interests of California in a general plan for improvement of the public highways, which will have the co-operation of all taxpayers and officials of the State.

Second. Such plan to include the procuring of legislation by the law-making body of the State of California, that will provide for the participation by the State government in the preliminary location, surveying and platting of a comprehensive system of roads for the State and the appropriation of a fair proportion of the funds necessary for the construction of the same, and to secure for such purpose a fair proportion of such moneys as may be appropriated by the national government for public road building, and by it apportioned to the State of California.

Third. Preserving the original government road of Spanish California between the Missions San Diego and Solano de Sonoma, and recording the history and traditions of the road.

Fourth. Investigating the adaptability of portions of this road to the purposes of a main highway, with the twenty-one Franciscan Missions as stations and landmarks upon it.

Fifth. Securing surveys in each of the counties along this route of as much of this ancient road as is in existence, and connecting such surveys with surveys of practical extensions of such existing portions of said road, which will be in consonance with the scheme for a main highway for the entire length, and to have surveyed and platted other roads intersecting it, which are of sufficient importance to warrant their being included in the general plan of a State highway system.

Sixth. To make this main highway from San Diego to Solano de Sonoma Mission a memorial highway, preserving its Spanish name of El Camino Real and urging the building of an extension thereof from its northern terminus northerly through the Sacramento Valley to the northern limits of the State as a main highway.

Seventh. To create and foster interest in the ornamentation of the borders of public roads, and of the property abutting the same throughout the State, and to further by every possible means an interest in ornamental tree culture, floriculture and forestry within the State of California.

Excerpt from the announcement of the state convention in Santa Barbara.

ᔆ The Santa Barbara Convention ᑫ

According to reports, there were over ninety people at the Santa Barbara convention. They represented 26 cities and such civic organizations as the California Federation of Women's Clubs, Native Sons and Daughters of the Golden West, County Association of Women's Clubs, County Boards of Supervisors, and the Native Daughters Improvement Society. Most of the representatives were from south of the San Luis Obispo County line, giving the south an advantage in voting. Concern about this inequity was expressed by the northern delegation. But, as the meeting progressed, everyone seemed to be in harmony, and by the end of the second day a statewide organization was formed, the El Camino Real Association of California.

To put this new organization into action, a State Executive Committee of eighteen delegates was elected and given the power to elect a president, eight vice-presidents, a treasurer, a secretary, and two auditors. Mr. A. P. Flaming was the first president. Mrs. Caroline R. Olney was elected secretary, and Mrs. Forbes served as one of the auditors. One of the first responsibilities of the secretary was to organize the sections in the various counties through which El Camino Real passed. Sections were soon formed in Los Angeles, San Diego, Pasadena, and Ventura.

In the Twenty-third Annual Session of the Grand Parlor of the Native Daughters of the Golden West we find the following information concerning the Los Angeles section of the El Camino Real Association of California.

EL CAMINO REAL,
LOS ANGELES SECTION,
CONSTITUTION AND BY-LAWS
ARTICLE 1.

This association shall be known as Los Angeles Section No. 5 of the El Camino Real Association of California.[17]

How the numbering of the sections occurred is unknown. The names of the sections that have been mentioned in various documents are San Diego, Orange, Los Angeles, Ventura, Santa Barbara, San Luis Obispo, San Francisco, and Oakland.

At the April 1904 meeting in Santa Barbara, the newly-selected executive board charged the Los Angeles section with two distinct assignments, to investigate the route of El Camino Real, and to provide a distinctive, emblematic, and appropriate guide-post to mark this route.

₭ Funding the Project ℚ

The first attempt to raise funds for the preservation of El Camino Real began with Miss Pitcher soon after she conceived the idea. In 1884 Charles Lummis provided her with the Landmarks Club membership list, and there is speculation that she used this list wisely and efficiently to help sup-

17. NDGW Annual Report, 1909, pp. 390–391.

port her many projects. She was diligently attempting to develop her plan for saving El Camino Real by any means that she could find. Knowledge of her personal history and fund-raising activities from 1892–1902 are almost non-existent, but we do know that she raised funds for the first Pasadena library and other worthy causes through the Pasadena Exhibition Association. The CFWC "Biennial Guide" (Index of Spots of Interest) included the following:

EL CAMINO REAL
Official display of the
PASADENA EXHIBITION ASSOCIATION
in the Los Angeles Chamber of Commerce.
Resources, picturesqueness and artistic possibilities of a
road from San Diego, through Los Angeles and
San Francisco, to San Francisco Solano
The Exhibit will embrace two divisions outside of, yet
supplementing
the general Road Plan. These divisions are

LITERATURE AND ILLUSTRATION
and
CONNOISSEURSHIP IN COLLECTING[18]

The following page of the guide is devoted to thirteen companies that entered exhibits.[19] At the bottom of this page is a note stating that "A royalty on all orders taken for advertisers, by the Association, goes to support the plan of the Camino Real."

One of the exhibits was provided by C. C. Pierce and Company, whose ad states "Photographic Collections: Missions, El Camino Real, Ramona, Indian Baskets, Pasadena, Los Angeles." Their advertisement is of special interest in that it relates to the Forbeses. From December 1901 until 1906, Mr. Forbes, a photographer, was owner of the Platingraph Photo Manufacturing Company of Los Angeles. He used C. C. Pierce and Company as a retail sales outlet for his photos. Mrs. Forbes was also a photographer. She was on the Board of Directors of the Los Angeles Camera Club in 1901 and was the first woman exhibitor at

18. CFWC 1902 Biennial Guide, p. 32.
19. CFWC 1902 Biennial Guide, p 33.

the first Los Angeles Photographic Salon. Thus it is possible one or the other of them convinced C. C. Pierce to place the ad.[20]

Between 1902 and 1904 the subject of restoring El Camino Real was brought up many times at CFWC and NDGW meetings. There is no documentation from either organization indicating that funds were raised or that any type of permanent work was accomplished directly pertaining to preservation of El Camino Real. Both organizations did, however, accomplish outstanding work on the preservation of various missions.

It was only after the establishment of the state El Camino Real Association that concentrated efforts were made to raise funds. Once again the Landmarks Club membership records were made available, and Mrs. Forbes made good use of them by writing to every member (there were well over five hundred in various states of the union) asking for donations.

To assist in financing the work at hand, the newly formed Los Angeles section sought ways to raise money. The details of their first attempt are related by Phil Brigandi, curator of the Ramona Pageant Association:

> "Ramona" was presented at the Mason Opera House in Los Angeles on February 27, 28, and March 1, 1905. The dramatization was written by Johnstone Jones and Virginia Calhoun who played the title role. Her Alessandro, incidentally, was D. W. Griffith, who later produced the first motion picture version of "Ramona" (filmed in Ventura County in 1910).[21]

The program for these performances states that "this presentation of RAMONA is given in Los Angeles under the auspices of the Los Angeles Section, EL CAMINO REAL ASSOCIATION."

20. When some of the Forbeses' old photographs were auctioned in 1994, it was difficult to distinguish the photographer since little is known of their history. In the Pacific Book Auction Galleries "Fine Western Americana" catalog, February 24, 1994, it is stated: "Among the exhibitors at the [1901] Salon were Mrs. A. S. C. Forbes." Upon close examination of the signatures on the back of all of the photographs, your authors found that the photos were, in fact, the work of her husband, A. S. C. Forbes. Mrs. Forbes was by far the better-remembered in California history, thus the mistaken assumption that they were her work.

21. Letter to the author, December 10, 1991.

❦ Tracing the Route ❧

A committee was appointed to study the old roads, trace El Camino Real, and report its findings to the state executive committee. From 1904 to 1905 the Los Angeles section was completely engaged in documenting, as closely as possible, the "original" route of El Camino Real. Initially, only that part of the road passing through Los Angeles, Orange, and San Diego Counties was researched. In 1905 the road committee reported to the state executive committee: "[The] Los Angeles section had an abstract and map of all old roads in Los Angeles and Orange counties, made for them by the Title Indemnity and Trust Company."

During 1905 to 1906, the road investigation was expanded from Los Angeles to Sonoma. Road routes were verified from a variety of sources, including church records, land grants of ranchos, and invaluable information furnished by old Spanish families and pioneers. A second report to the state executive committee stated, ". . . there is not one mile of the old road that was not investigated by the Road Committee."[22]

❦ Designing the Bells ❧

In 1906 the executive board of the Los Angeles section decided to mark El Camino Real with a distinctive and appropriate emblem. Mrs. Forbes submitted her design, a mission bell on a standard with a guide board giving directions and information concerning the missions. This was accepted, and she secured a design patent and copyright. While we know that a Mrs. C. F. Gates came up with the original idea of a bell, historical records are silent as to details about Mrs. Gates and her part in this story beyond this. However, in the Twenty-forth Annual Session of the Grand Parlor, Mrs. Forbes says: "Upon the suggestion of Mrs. Gates, I designed this sign post. . . ."[23]

22. Although these reports were widely distributed, the authors have not been able to find a single copy.

23. NDGW Annual Report, 1910, p. 173.

There are conflicting reports concerning which bell served as inspiration for the El Camino Real bell design. The *Santa Barbara Morning Press* for August 14, 1906, claimed without documentation, "Replica of the Early Santa Barbara Bell Adopted by the El Camino Real Association." Because the bells have become so popular, public speculation on how the bell design was chosen has created some vivid stories. By far the most popular is that Mrs. Forbes created the bell design for a contest held by the El Camino Real Association. No evidence of such a "contest" has been found. However, Mrs. Forbes leaves no doubt concerning the model for her bell design. She finalized her sketches while looking at the bells in the Old Plaza Church in Los Angeles. It is worth noting that a measurement of the bells at Mission Santa Barbara would have shown that none of the bells were the same size or proportion as the El Camino Real bells.

On the side of the first bell, which was erected at the Plaza Church in Los Angeles, we find the dates 1769 and 1906. These dates refer to the founding of the first mission (San Diego) and the erection of the first El Camino Real bell (Los Angeles). Around the bell's bottom rim and directly below the dates are the words EL CAMINO REAL. On the back of the bell around the lip is an inscription in 1/2 inch letters, "PATENT AND COPYRIGHT 1906 BY MRS. A.S.C. FORBES." Mrs. Miriam Nichols of the Vista Woman's Club, working through the copyright office, found the following verification of the copyright: "EL CAMINO REAL; by Mrs. Armitage S. C. Forbes. Entered in the name of Mrs. Armitage S. C. Forbes under F 48165, December 4, 1906; two copies received December 4, 1906."

No other lettering is on the bell. Each bell weighed approximately ninety-two pounds, and hung on a post of bent one-and-a-half inch diameter piping that fitted into a larger base pipe mounted in concrete. The post was eleven feet high and could easily be seen by a passing traveler. Some posts displayed a brass plate with the donor's name and date. Some of these plates can still be seen at various locations today.

Everything about this bell was symbolic. In *California Missions and Landmarks El Camino Real* Mrs. Forbes elaborates on the design.

> In selecting the Bell as an appropriate marker for the road of the missions the fact was taken into consideration that at all times the padres first hung a bell that they might

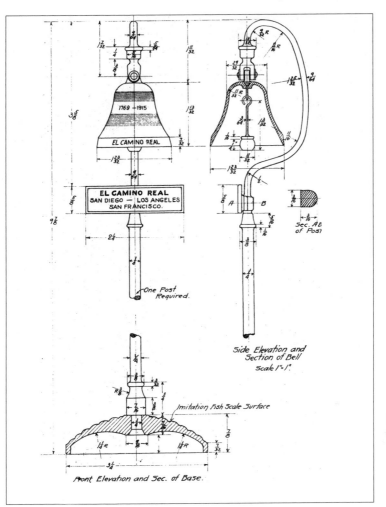

Blueprint of one of the miniature replica bells produced by Mrs. Forbes, showing the standard and plaque.

call attention to the work in hand, that of erecting and blessing the cross; the Bell guideposts were erected to call attention to the work in hand, that of reconstructing El Camino Real, the road of the missions. Iron was selected for the material from which to construct the bells for the reason that the entire proposition to reconstruct El Camino Real is one of emblematic sentiment and the iron is intended to represent the iron will of the men who made

First El Camino Real bell in front of the Plaza Church in Los Angeles.

the first roads in California. The Bell guide-post is of plain, severe design to represent the simple, austere life led by these men of God. Brass or tinkling metal was intentionally not used, as the bell is intended as a memorial tribute to the work and lives of the Franciscan friars.[24]

The task of placing the bells was given to the newly created bell committee composed of A. S. C. Forbes, chair; Reverend Juan Caballeria; and B. H. Cass.

---

24. A. S. C. Forbes, *California Missions and Landmarks*, third edition (1915), pp. 275-77.

THE BELLS BECOME
A REALITY

El Camino Real
LOS ANGELES SECTION

O. SHEPARD BARNUM
President

GEN. ROBT. WANKOWSKI
Treasurer

COL. J. B. LANKERSHIM
Vice-President

MRS. A. S. C. FORBES
Secretary

Reopening of El Camino Real

Dedication of Bells by

Father Juan Caballeria

You are cordially invited to be present at the ceremony of the dedication of the bells marking the old historic road of El Camino Real to be held at the Church of Nuestra Senora Reina de Los Angeles, at the Plaza, Wednesday, August 15th, 1906.

Dedication and erection of Bell 11 A. M.

Mrs A S C Forbes
Secretary.

Invitation to the dedication of the first El Camino Real bell.

On August 15, 1906, at the Plaza Church in downtown Los Angeles, the first of a series of bells was erected. According to Forbes

67

The first bell was erected and dedicated August 15th, 1906 at the Plaza Church, Los Angeles, as a part of the festival to commemorate the feast of Nuestra Señora la Reina de Los Angeles. . . Rev. Juan Caballeria, rector of the Plaza Church, delivered the opening address.[25]

The second bell to be erected was located at Mission San Diego. During the second bell installation, also in 1906, the stand was dedicated and named the "Jayme stand" for the first martyred Franciscan friar, Father Luis Jayme, who was killed in the first native uprising in San Diego, November 4, 1775.

After this, bells began to appear throughout southern California. "The bells proved to be an inspiration. After fifty-four bells had been erected south of the Santa Barbara County line the work was then extended northward."[26]

An idea of the pattern of bell distribution can be gleaned from a letter, dated May 15, 1914, from the El Camino Real Association of California, Mrs. Forbes, to Miss Ida Blaine, recording secretary of Reina del Mar Parlor, NDGW:

> request made by Mr. Forbes for three bells from the Chamber of Commerce of Santa Barbara and the location of same. We wish the bells to be placed at E. Boulevard and State Street and Hollister Avenue, the other about a mile to the south-east on the corner of Boulevard and State Street. . . .

> Mr. Forbes leaves in a day or two to oversee the erection of 19 bells for the city of San Diego, that will make 75 Bells for San Diego County and City.

> Santa Barbara County and for Ventura the Supervisors have agreed to order 35 or 40 Bells after June 1st which is the end of the fiscal year.

> It will take 50 bells for Santa Barbara Co. 3 for the city and this will make a continuous chain of almost a Bell a mile from Mission San Diego to the northern County line of Santa Barbara.

25. A. S. C. Forbes, *California Missions and Landmarks*, third edition (1915), p. 277.

26. A. S. C. Forbes, *California Missions and Landmarks*, third edition (1915), p. 278.

Delivery of bells for San Diego, circa 1910.

The concept of one bell for each mile was more an ideal than a reality. According to 1912 road maps, the distance from Mission San Diego to Santa Barbara City was 236 miles. The total distance from San Diego to San Francisco was 603.7 miles (not including the unrecorded mileage to Sonoma, which was approximately 50 miles). Because of city, county, and state regulations, El Camino Real bells could not be located randomly along the roadside. In some locations, such as Los Angeles, a permit was required. For example, on February 11, 1914, Mrs. Forbes was granted Permit No. 9 from the California Highway Department.

During Governor Ronald Reagan's term in office, he requested an inventory of all bells on El Camino Real. The final report submitted by Caltrans showed that 128 El Camino Real bells could still be found on state highways. This report did not include city or county roads. At the dawn of the twenty-first century we can estimate a total of over 380 bells now in place marking the historic El Camino Real and its branches.

ଔ Casting the Bells ଔ

Who made the bells? It is a popular belief that Mrs. Forbes herself cast the bells after approval of the El Camino Real Association executive committee. This cannot be historically supported. Several times in her correspondence Mrs. Forbes cites "bells on order." This could mean she was ordering them from a foundry. We recently found information in the CFWC archives at the University of California, Santa Cruz, that clears up where these first bells were cast. "These stan-

Mrs. A. S. C. Forbes in her Los Angeles display room with some of her bells. (Courtesy Campo de Cahuenga Historical Memorial Association)

dards and bells are sold by the Pacific Sign and Enameling Company, La Grande and Mateo streets, Los Angeles."[27] How long this company supplied the standards and bells is unknown but this would explain the "bells on order" phrase. We should note here that occasionally throughout our research, we have come across references to a foundry operated by the Forbeses or a foundry in which Mrs. Forbes had part interest. There are also references to a foundry owned by her husband. It does seem, however, that they did at some

27. California Federation of Women's Clubs Annual Report 1908–1909, p. 55.

time operate a foundry. Mrs. Forbes has been quoted in a few instances as saying that she was dismayed by the waste metal in the shop and was determined to find a way to put it to good use. Also, she was quoted as saying she had always loved bells and learned all she could about them, their design, metal content, and history.

A *Los Angeles Times* article of Feb. 8, 1935, begins: "With another Easter in the offing, the bellmaker of Los Angeles yesterday began shipment of toned replicas of historic mission bells." It then continues with: "The bells are made in the foundry of Mrs. A. S. C. Forbes at 335 West Thirty-First Street." An accompanying photo is captioned, "Within the only foundry of its kind in the United States, Cecelia Parker sounds out one of the old California mission bells manufactured there. Mrs. A. S. C. Forbes, owner of the foundry, is shown with her." Strangely, the *Times* gives no name for the business.

We know that in 1914 the Forbeses owned the Novelty Manufacturing Company at a different address in Los Angeles. By 1922 they had moved the business to the West Thirty-First Street address. The name Novelty Manufacturing does not bring to mind the image of a foundry casting 1,800-pound bells, as has been claimed in several sources; however, we can be sure that this was the source for the many miniature bells she sold.

Other sources claim that the Forbeses made El Camino Real bells in their own foundry, the California Bell Company. While available records do not bear this out, we think it is highly likely that, at some time, they did make the large bells. We do not know when the business name changed.

From all evidence that we have been able to gather, Mr. Forbes made bells in his "foundry shop." We know neither the location nor the date. In 1914 they started making miniatures at the Novelty Manufacturing Company. In 1928 Mr. Forbes passed away and Mrs. Forbes took over the business. She has been quoted as saying in 1936, "I suppose I have made hundreds of thousands of bells since I first began twenty-eight years ago. This sounds like a tremendously large figure but a great many of these were tiny souvenir bells—replicas of the bells that hang in the Southern California missions."[28] The quote would seem to indicate that Mr. and

28. *Los Angeles Times Sunday Magazine*, October 18, 1936.

Mrs. Forbes were, indeed, somehow involved with a foundry in 1908.

From the time of her husband's death until 1948, Mrs. Forbes operated the business by herself. She insisted that a woman operate her foundry after she left.

Evangeline Aldrich and Mae Franklin, the two women who purchased the Novelty Manufacturing Company, continued to sell the same line of bells that Mrs. Forbes had made famous. We have unsubstantiated information that they ordered bells from foundries for installation on El Camino Real, along with desk bells and other miniatures, doing the finish work themselves.

They continued until 1951 when they sold to Mr. J. Rice of Los Angeles.[29] His catalog featured pictures of a number of Mrs. Forbes's original bells, from a hefty thirty-five pounds to only a few ounces. The back page of the catalog offered the following: "authentic reproductions made world famous by Mrs. A. S. C. Forbes now made exclusively by the California Bell Company. For over thirty years, reproductions of early California mission bells have been Souvenir and Collectors items." On the front page was the prominent name California Bell Company. Mr. Rice did not cast any bells for placement along El Camino Real. He employed two sales representatives, Laurette Ebbett and Edward Hardy. Bell sales were extremely good and it looked like the company would prosper, but after an unfortunate partnership and events beyond Rice's control, he closed the company in 1964. As happens so often, the records and equipment were lost.

Mrs. Forbes's death in 1951 ended an era that saw great work and dedication in the designation, preservation, and marking of El Camino Real of California. From 1951 to 1959 El Camino Real bells were cast by various foundries and installed by civic- and historic-minded organizations. Information about this time is sketchy, when available at all. We have been unable to ascertain the names of the foundries doing the work during these years.

In 1959 the California Department of Transportation needed bells to replace the ones destroyed by roadwork and taken by vandals. Not having a source, they sent foundries and bell designers an invitation to bid on a bell. This bell

---

29. Mr. Rice informed us that the name of the business he bought was the California Bell Company and that he kept that name.

design was awarded to an unidentified foundry near Fresno, California. Two variations of this bell were cast. However, it is not known how many were produced.

Finally, in 1960, Justin Kramer of Los Angeles won the bid on a new style of bell. His design has become the standard on El Camino Real, and he is still casting these famous road markers into the twenty-first century. Justin Kramer changed the dating on his bells to recognize the "International Heritage Corridor" in 1997.

❧ Mystery Bells ❧

What the first bell was like can only be the subject of speculation. Did the design by Mrs. Forbes have an inscription? We do not have valid information to confirm any inscriptions. Mrs. Forbes is silent on that point until August of 1906. No record of bell inscriptions can be located in the many letters, notes, and other correspondence by the Forbeses prior to 1906. From all written accounts the first bell, with inscriptions, was installed in Los Angeles in 1906.

Is it possible that there were bells cast and installed prior to August 1906 that bore no inscriptions? If so, that would help explain the "Forbes type" bells that have been showing up from time to time with no inscription. Mrs. Forbes designed a series of El Camino Real bells, most for installation on El Camino Real. The lone exception is the "Landmarks" bell. Forbes had a copyright on the wording *El Camino Real*, preventing usage for other than El Camino Real bells. Possibly the "no inscription" bells were used for marking sites not connected with a landmark or El Camino Real. At the end of a *San Diego Union* article concerning the August 15, 1906, Plaza Church dedication, the writer quotes from an unknown source, "Twenty bells have been installed . . . to the Ventura County line."[30] To further confuse the issue, the *San Jose Mercury News*, August 28, 1991, recounting a 1905 Fourth of July celebration in Irvington, published a picture showing a bell which can be plainly identified as a "Forbes bell." These two articles could be written off as a misprint if it were not for a personal scrapbook belonging to a Mrs. A. F. Anderson of Irvington. This family scrapbook contains

30. *San Diego Union*, August 16, 1906.

a photograph of the same event, showing the bell from a different angle. She also has an invitation to the celebration, which her parents had saved along with the picture. She assured us that her picture and invitation came from the 1905 section of the scrapbook.

This is mystifying because Mrs. Forbes herself states very clearly in her book that the first bell was installed in Los Angeles in 1906. Did she mean the very first bell or the first bell with an inscription? We feel that, quite possibly, bells were produced and used for reasons other than marking El Camino Real before Mrs. Forbes acquired the copyright. These mystery bells are located presently in various locations both on and away from El Camino Real. We know of four in San Diego. Mrs. Forbes sold her foundry in 1948. Possibly the new owners produced bells without inscriptions, but that would not account for a Forbes bell in Irvington in 1905. We can only leave this subject with questions unanswered and continue our story.

❧ The Cost of the Bells ❧

It is often asked how much the bells cost. The California Federation of Women's Clubs annual report of 1906–1907 related that "the bells are secured at a cost of $19.50 each."[31]

The Native Daughters of the Golden West provide us with a detailed cost breakdown in the report on their Twenty-fourth Annual Session (1910):

> The cost of placing a Mission Bell sign post is as follows: the sign post, bell (all metal) and the markers, complete, as sent out from the foundry in Los Angeles, cost $25. The freight is about $2, the concrete base from $2 to $8, according to size and shape. The sum of $35 would cover all costs.[32]

In the 1950s Mrs. Eileen Dismuke of Santa Barbara took on the task of administering placement of El Camino Real bells. She organized the Committee of El Camino Real and,

---

31. CFWC Annual Report, 1906–1907, p. 29.

32. Report of the 24th Annual Session of the NDGW Grand Parlor, 1910, p. 203.

in order to offset the expense to the clubs, obtained contributions to cover the cost of the bells only. She shed light on the cost of the bells in her 1963 report to the NDGW Grand Parlor: "A purchase price of $25.00, which was at a cost basis, was secured from a Los Angeles Bell Manufacturing Company, who furnished the bells at cost price as a public relations venture because of their great interest in the program."[33]

In the 1965 annual report to the NDGW Grand Parlor she reported: "These bells may be secured by contacting me, the only expense to a Parlor requesting a bell being that of purchase of a standard for the bell, at a cost of $35.00 plus installation expense."[34]

When Mrs. Dismuke reported to the NDGW Grand Parlor in 1974, the following prices were noted: "While the cost in 1959 when the first bell was placed [by the Committee of El Camino Real] at $25.00, the cost of replacement now is $110.00."[35]

The present cost of the Justin Kramer bell and standard provided by the California Federation of Women's Club's project is $1,000. This new type of bell, provided by the CFWC's Adopt-A-Bell Program, is designed to be "theft proof."

๛ Maintaining the Bells ⊂⊃

Unfortunately, since the installation of the first bell, no provision had been made for their upkeep, and over the years deterioration took its toll on these historic highway markers. In 1913 Supervisor J. Emmet Hayden, who represented the Native Sons of the Golden West in the El Camino Real Association, sent a letter to the state Board of Public Works asking that it do its share in maintaining the mission bells along El Camino Real in preparation for the 1915 Pan American Exhibition. "The mission bells along El Camino Real all the way from San Francisco to San Diego

33. NDGW Annual Report, 1963, p. 328.
34. NDGW Annual Report, 1965, p. 299
35. NDGW Annual Report, 1974, p. 246.

California State Automobile Association road and sign repair truck. (Courtesy California State Automobile Association)

are to be repainted and generally restored and numerous new ones are to be placed. . . ." Although this work was never accomplished, it is the first mention of the early bells being painted.

In 1926 the El Camino Real Association appealed to the Automobile Club of Southern California (ACSC) and to the CSAA to take on the maintenance of El Camino Real bells. After twenty years of neglect, the bells had become quite unsightly. The only exception was the bell and standard placed in front of the Plaza Church in Los Angeles, which had been painted. Assuming this new responsibility, the two automobile clubs provided regular maintenance of the bells, probably in conjunction with maintenance of the roads and signs on the bell posts, painting them the familiar green color we see today. From 1926 to 1931, the CSAA, in conjunction with the ACSC, took on the task of maintaining the mission bell markers along state-owned property from Sonoma to San Diego.

These markers played a vital role in directing California motorists in the early part of the century. We must remember that no map existed for the entire length of El Camino Real until 1912, when the American Automobile Association

Automobile Club of Southern California service truck outside their headquarters. (Courtesy Automobile Club of Southern California)

published a series of strip (or section) maps for the entire road. These maps represented a monumental project for that time, and marked the beginning of AAA map service for the California motorist.

⅏ Locations Beyond El Camino Real ⚝

Shortly after the first bell was erected in 1906, the CFWC and the NDGW began raising funds and placed a great many bells along sections of El Camino Real. However, bell placement has not been limited entirely to El Camino Real, nor even to California.

In 1963 Mr. and Mrs. George Whitney of Upland purchased a Justin Kramer bell which they presented to the museum at the birthplace of Junípero Serra in Majorca, Spain. The Whitneys relate the event in an undated letter to the author. Their account of this gift is as follows.

> Mr. and Mrs. George H. Whitney with their two daughters, Mary Catherine and Olive Therese, while visiting Petra, Majorca, Spain, met and visited with Dina Moore Bowded who was the inspiring Californian living on the island and whose interest was the birthplace and museum

El Camino Real bell at the San Ysidro/Tijuana border crossing.

of Fray Junípero Serra. She was interested in obtaining [an] El Camino Real bell for the entrance of the museum. After numerous requests of many prominent persons throughout the state, she finally asked the Whitneys and the Whitneys were able to up and deliver [a bell] to the Museum where it now stands. The Whitney bell was the only gift that Serra received on the 250th anniversary of his birth. Many Californians are pleasantly surprised to find the California El Camino Real bell in Petra.

To this date, three international bells have been installed in Baja California, helping to commemorate the "Heritage Corridor," El Camino Real, in that part of Mexico. The first was erected in 1996 in Loreto, Baja California Sur, commemorating the 300th anniversary of the establishment of the first successful permanent mission in the Californias, and marking the starting point of El Camino Real. The second

El Camino Real bell near La Misión, Baja California, Mexico.

was placed in a colorful ceremony as two nations joined hands in friendship on the U.S./Mexico border at Tijuana in June 1998. In July 1999, a third bell was installed on Mexico Highway 1 beside the northbound lane near the village of La Misión in Baja California.

❧ The UCB Bells ❦

In a special report on the El Camino Real bell program initiated by the United California Bank, in cooperation with parlors of the NDGW, Eileen Dismuke, Native Daughters representative on the statewide committee for El Camino Real, states:

In the fall of 1969 your speaker was invited to attend the ground breaking of a new 14-story United California Bank, in Encino in the San Fernando Valley area of Los Angeles County, located on Ventura Boulevard and the original route of the El Camino Real Highway.

The purpose and significance of this ground breaking was that the bank, in recognition of the bicentennial celebrations of California's Mission Chain, had decided to have an El Camino Real bell placed in a prominent place in front of this new building when it was completed in February 1971 to denote its location on the El Camino Real. The President of the United California Bank, with other state, county, and local dignitaries, was impressed with the historic significance of the El Camino Real Bells. As a result, the bank, at a subsequent meeting of its Board of Directors decided, as a public relations gesture in recognition of the bicentennial, to place an El Camino Real Bell at each of the twenty-eight new banks contemplated by United California Bank along the El Camino Real, from San Diego to San Francisco and east to San Rafael.

Working to save El Camino Real was only one of the many achievements of Mrs. Dismuke. She was the one who contacted the United California Bank (UCB) and persuaded them to use the El Camino Real bell as a symbol. As a result, UCB purchased more than twenty-eight bells and had them installed at new branches throughout the state. Eventually the number of bells placed in front of the banks grew to thirty-four.

UCB has a long history in California. It was founded in 1873 as the Gold Bank of Santa Barbara. A few years later the name was changed to First National Bank of Santa Barbara. In 1948 the seventy-fifth anniversary of the original bank was celebrated but with a new name: Trust and Savings of Santa Barbara. To commemorate that anniversary, small bells were cast by Mrs. A. S. C. Forbes for the bank to use in publicity. The passing years saw a series of buyouts, name changes, and so on, until, finally, UCB was established.

THE ADOPT-A-BELL PROJECT

Display of El Camino Real bells and artifacts at the Ventura County Museum of Art and History, 1992.

ഉറ

A s has been described earlier, placement of bells along the historic El Camino Real during the twentieth century has been an ongoing project of the CFWC and the NDGW. These two organizations have dedicated their time and effort to saving El Camino Real, marking this historic road, pushing legislation through the California legislature for the protection of the bells, and making El Camino Real safe for drivers.

However, at times enthusiasm waned. Few bells were installed following Mrs. Forbes's death in 1950. It seemed the entire bell placement program, and possibly El Camino Real itself, would be forgotten. Old civic buildings were demolished

81

and the bells at their entrances disappeared. New roads were designed, built, numbered, and named. No organization was actively engaged in salvaging the bells and standards as they were bulldozed over during highway construction.

Luckily, during the last decade of the twentieth century an ambitious program to install new Camino Real bells along the historic road was promoted by Mrs. Sandy Morgan, state president of the California Federation of Women's Clubs. Mrs. Morgan's program involved the CFWC and the automobile clubs of California, California government offices and departments, city and county governments of those communities situated on El Camino Real, Caltrans districts and personnel, and U.S. Government offices. Through the efforts of the California Department of Transportation, more than twenty states, Canada, and Puerto Rico are aware of the Adopt-A-Bell project. To say it was a tremendous success would be an understatement.

The inspiration for this project was a 1992 exhibit held at the Ventura County Museum of Art and History. The display of "The Bells of El Camino Real," along with the miniature El Camino Real bells, coincided with the annual meetings of the NDGW and CFWC in Ventura. Each organization held a reception at the museum, as did the Automobile Club of Southern California. During the CFWC reception Mrs. Morgan expressed her excitement about the display, saying that when she became state president, replacing the bells on El Camino Real would be the federation's project.

During her inauguration speech in 1996, Mrs. Morgan made her plans clear:

> The [El Camino Real] mission bells will be the symbol . . . As the President's Special Project of this Administration, the CFWC, in a cooperative effort with the California Department of Transportation, and with MAJOR cosponsorship from the Automobile Clubs of California, will restore this chapter of California heritage through the CFWC Adopt-A-Bell project. . . . I have heard it said each president should leave her mark. I am more interested in the CFWC leaving ITS mark. Our mothers and grandmothers carried the torch for us; we must do nothing less for our daughters and granddaughters. So, together, we're going to leave OUR mark as we close a century of accomplishment.

Shortly after her inauguration, Sandy Morgan resigned her position. She was replaced by Mrs. Jeri Boone, who took up the cause and has ably led the CFWC in its ongoing projects.

The first bell of the Adopt-A-Bell project was dedicated July 12, 1996, in Santa Clara. This initial bell dedication in Santa Clara was to be the first of a series of bell placements that far exceeded the expectations of all involved.

This was a monumental project, extending from the Sonoma, East Bay, and San Francisco areas, along El Camino Real, touching the many missions, then on to San Diego. It expanded inland to San Fernando, San Gabriel, Riverside, and Imperial counties. The women joined forces and, with an overwhelming show of support and cooperation, researched history, raised funds, selected sites, and prevailed upon the local governments to install these historic symbols. Many of the city and county administrations were taken by surprise. Some of these government officials were unaware of the significance of the bells until members of CFWC, in official meetings, explained their unique history. These efforts culminated in research, education, and collaboration with historical societies and local governments to identify and mark their sections of this first California road. The chair for this statewide project is Mrs. Maureen Everett of San Jose, and a more competent and dynamic leader could not have been found.[36]

From 1996 to 2000 the CFWC identified portions of El Camino Real in the Californias that were never before acknowledged. The CFWC also reached across the international border into Mexico and shared in the recognition of El Camino Real in Baja California.

---

36. Your author, Max Kurillo, was given the honor of serving as historical consultant on this project. Working with Maureen Everett and CFWC President Mrs. Jeri Boone has been a profound and memorable pleasure.

EL CAMINO REAL AND THE
BELLS OF VENTURA COUNTY

Cars on the treacherous Casita Pass Road. (Courtesy Ventura County Museum)

M any counties in California can claim portions of El Camino Real, but one county has supported two Royal Roads. Both follow the trail (or road) from the earliest recorded period and maintain El Camino Real bell markers very close to the original routes. This county is Ventura.

On the first published map of California's El Camino Real for the motorist and traveler, published by the American Automobile Association in 1912, we find that El Camino Real followed old Ventura Boulevard in Los Angeles County to about Topanga Canyon. Here the macadam surfacing ended and the graded dirt road began. The road then traveled through Calabasas and on to Ventura County. The graded dirt road passed by the Newbury Park post office and, three miles farther, turned right to the approach of the Conejo (Spanish for *rabbit*) Pass, winding down its switchbacks with little more than one lane. The road then crossed the Southern Pacific rails and passed through Camarillo and El Rio, then crossed the Santa Clara River and continued on Conejo Road (now Ventura Boulevard) into the town of San Buenaventura.

During the 1800s, El Camino Real departed Mission San Buenaventura, turned to the right and followed Cañada Street (now Ventura Avenue), staying on the east side of the river. There was a crossing just above where Coyote Creek comes into the Ventura River. From this crossing a graded dirt road climbed uphill to the East Casitas Pass at about 1,155 feet. From there the road dropped to 1,000 feet at the West Casitas Pass, and continued on about four miles to Shepherd's Inn, where it entered Santa Barbara County. The entire route through Ventura County was a graded dirt road until about 1912. In the early and mid-1800s it was nothing but a wide horse and walking trail. Only after the advent of buggies, stagecoaches, and automobiles was the road widened and graded.

Prior to 1910, conditions on the Casitas Pass during any type of rain were terrible: the road was easily reduced to a muddy quagmire. As the *Ventura Democrat* stated in 1907, "The cities are not connected now by any thing that we may call a road. The old Casitas grade is a wreck and something must be done to make travel between the two cities [Ventura and Santa Barbara] possible."

Understandably, reports of this type discouraged many travelers from using that route. The historical alternative, beach travel for stage and wagon, continued. The beach route had been used from the time of the missions, but it also had drawbacks. Passage was restricted to low tide and daylight hours. The constantly moving rocks and wet sand made the beach route almost as treacherous as the mud of the Casitas Camino Real. As more people moved into Ventura County, increasing the demands on roads, the idea of building a wooden road around and near the place called Rincon gained momentum. To build such a road, however, would cost a huge sum of money.

The El Camino Real Association held the lead in the fund raising for this Ventura County project which would benefit the entire state. The association raised funds from private donations and from the proceeds of benefit performances of *Ramona*, presented at the Mason Opera House in Los Angeles on February 27, 28, and March 1, 1905.

Funds came from many other sources. In 1911 the El Camino Real Association presented a benefit for the Rincon Road. This benefit, given by the Stock Company, featured Mr. Nat C. Goodwin and Miss Marjorie Rambeau in *The Gilded Fool*, on August 28 and 29, 1911. The slogan for the event was, "Casitas Pass Overcome—Help hang the bell on Rincon sea-level road."

Many workmen donated their time to build a wooden road along the Rincon. This unique elevated wooden road, or causeway, ran along a section of some of the most beautiful coast in California. It also presented problems. During heavy surf and very high tides, the supports for this wooden road would wash out and automobiles had to make it on their own through the mud and wet sand. But now, in good weather, automobiles could travel from Ventura to Santa Barbara in about an hour and a half. The boards were rough and noisy but there was no comparison to the previous stagecoach rides through Ventura County. There are accounts of

The result of wave and storm action on the beach route between Santa Barbara and Ventura. (Courtesy Ventura County Museum)

The Rincon causeway. (Courtesy Ventura County Museum)

stage luggage being swept away while crossing the rivers in Ventura County, and of passengers being rescued by passing horsemen.

It would not be until December 21, 1972, that the Rincon route (7.9 miles in length) would be formally dedicated as part of Highway 101, and incorporated as a section of historic El Camino Real. The El Camino Real Association made provisions to mark this new section with approximately twenty bells.

℞ El Camino Real in Ventura County ℞

On December 3, 1903, a committee composed of Mrs. B. T. Williams, Mrs. W. H. Layne, Mrs. H. F. Clark, Mrs. L. B. Hogue, Mrs. J. B. Wagner, Mrs. J. A. Walker, Mrs. J. B. Alvord, Mrs. D. S. Blackburn, and Mrs. M. E. Dudley appeared before the Board of Supervisors of Ventura County. They urged the board to establish and recognize El Camino Real. The very next day, December 4, 1903, the County of

Ventura organized its first highway commission, composed of fifty-one people representing a stable cross-section of businessmen, laborers, farmers, and inspired citizens.

Of the many dedicated organizations involved in local and state history, the Landmarks Club of California stands out as one of the leaders. This club pushed for the recognition of California's history and for the establishment of landmarks of which Ventura County could be justifiably proud. The club's relentless leader was none other than Charles Lummis. On June 22, 1904, Lummis wrote (partly in Spanish) in his diary, "Voy a Plaza, meeting plan committee Camino Real Assn. Borden, Arnott, Mrs. Olney, Flemming."

On June 25, 1904, Charles Lummis came to the city of Ventura and spoke at the Opera House in an effort to organize a committee to take an active interest in Ventura County and effect a permanent El Camino Real organization. The following names appeared in the *Democrat* on June 25, 1904, as being "selected" by Lummis:[37]

Hon. Marion Cannon	Mrs. W. H. Lane
Mrs. M. E. Dudley	Mr. Albert Maulhardt
Mrs. D. S. Blackburn	Hon. H. Warring
Hon. T. G. Gabbert	Hon. D. T. Perkins
Miss Seymore (of Briggs)	Mrs. B. T. Williams
Mrs. Alice McKevett	Mrs. Ella C. Orr
Mrs. John B. Wagner	Mrs. E. P. Foster
Mrs. Harriet A. Berry	Mrs. John A. Walker
Mrs. T. R. Bard	

These individuals, it is to be assumed, were the people who made up the Ventura County section of the El Camino Real Association.

A January 28, 1904, article in the *Democrat* alerted readers to an upcoming chamber of commerce meeting in Los Angeles to ". . . form a plan for the construction of the El Camino Real . . . it is to be hoped that Ventura county will be represented."

On March 30, 1904, the same newspaper informed readers of the Santa Barbara meeting to plan for the construction of El Camino Real. Ventura was well represented during the organizational meeting in Santa Barbara in April

37. *Ventura Daily Democrat*, June 26, 1904.

1904. Attendees included Mrs. M. E. Dudley, California Federation of Women's Clubs; Mrs. Orpha W. Foster, president, County Association of Women's Clubs; T. G. Gabbert, chair, County Board of Supervisors; and Mrs. B. T. Williams, Native Daughters Improvement Society.

In January 1904 the *Democrat* assured the people of Ventura County that

> There is no doubt that Ventura will do her part to further the plan, as the line traces the very center of the most populous section of the county, and it is not necessary to describe in words what that means to the people thus benefited. Camino Real would be the greatest advertisement the whole state could have, as it would become known and be discussed in every civilized country on the globe.

On June 23, 1904, a poem by Mrs. M. E. Dudley appeared in the *Democrat*:

ᔖᑕᐯ
Uncle Nathan Talks About the Camino Real

I've heard they think to build a road in California State,
To run the whole blame length of it, for passengers and freight,
That's why their holdin' all around, conventions, where folks
  show,
How much they need the plaguey thing, and try to make it go.
Now this Camino Real has a master name I think,
It's one o' them the Padres gave and takes a sight o' ink,
But if they'd call it just plain road it wouldn't do I hear,
For folks are great on sentiment and want the title clear.
I hope they'll hustle matters up, and when it's done, some day,
I guess I'll take a little ride with Ma, behind Old Grey.
The trees and flow'rs and shrubs and things, will be a purty
  sight,
Au-tom-obles and kerrages will each have room to light.
For they intend to make it broad as well as long they say,
'Twill be so mighty splendid now a reg'lar King's Highway,
I wonder what the Padres think who first this road surveyed,
To see the pesky Protestants a takin' of their grade.
I've always been a hearin' since I was 'bout knee-high,
that Catholics and Protestants don't mingle in the sky,
But times out here are changin' and thoughts and roads grow
  broad,

Because the folks that's livin' now all worship the same God.
I hope they'll raise the money and start the thing all right,
I'll give a shillin' towards it if fee-nances are tight,
Fer Ma and me way down in Main have made a little "pile",
And we ain't no ways graspin' but like the Western style.
Of startin' into things that's big and carryin' of em through,
And git the whole blame business done, while we could set a
    screw,
Here's fer Camino Real, I'll wish her well agin,
Whoever pays and prays fer her, I'll allus say—Amen!

&0C8

On December 7, 1906, the Ventura County Board of
Supervisors agreed to install ten El Camino Real bells at
selected locations. The supervisors would buy three: The other
seven were to be purchased by others. By the time the bells
were purchased and arrangements were made for installation,
it was February 1907. At the February 12, 1907, meeting of
the Ventura Board of Supervisors, the County Surveyor was
instructed

> to place on the map heretofore made designation the places
> at which El Camino Real Bells are to be placed, the angles
> at which said signs are to stand and the distances between
> points to be placed on said signs.[38]

By 1907, Ventura was one of the leading counties in the
installation of El Camino Real bells. The Ventura County
Board of Supervisors took an active part, choosing twelve post
locations at the most important intersections on the highway.
In Ventura County all bell sign posts were to bear a brass
tablet or plate stating the name of the organization purchas-
ing the signpost. The supporting Ventura societies, the location, and number of bells were as follows:

Native Sons of the Golden West
West Main Street and Vista Avenue   1 bell
Native Daughters of the Golden West
Ventura Mission   1 bell
Tuesday Club
Two mi. from Ventura River at bridge   1 bell

38. Ventura County Supervisors, "Concerning Camino Real Sign Posts and
Bells," minutes of December 7, 1906, p. 38.

Wednesday Western Club of Mound
Two mi. from mission   1 bell
Society of Pioneers
Los Angeles County line   2 bells
I.N.S. of Briggs
Santa Barbara County line   1 bell
Ventura Board of Supervisors
Locations unknown   5 bells
Avenue Club
New bridge at river   1 bell
Camino Real Society of Ventura
Casitas Summit   1 bell

Other locations not identified with any particular organization were:

Borchard's ranch at Conejo	1 bell
on High Road on the long grade	1 bell
Camarillo	1 bell
Springville	1 bell
T. A. Rice's (junction of Conejo Road and Los Angeles Avenue)	1 bell
El Rio-Savier's and Conejo junction	1 bell
George Cook's place at the junction of the road leading to Saticoy	1 bell
Forks of the road two-and-one-half miles east from San Buenaventura	1 bell
Near the bridge two-and-one-half miles east of the mission	1 bell

In a 1910 El Camino Real Association report, Mrs. Forbes presented a list of counties and cities (and their donors) that had erected bells, including the following for Ventura County:

Native Daughters Improvement Club
Mission San Buenaventura
NDGW, Cabrillo Parlor
Ventura Ave., two blocks from mission
Tuesday Club of Ventura
One mile from mission
Wednesday Afternoon Club of Mound
Two miles from Mission Avenue
Ladies Club of Ventura
Foster Park at the stone bridge
Pioneer Society of Ventura

County line at Los Angeles
Pioneer Society of Ventura
County line at Santa Barbara
Ventura Board of Supervisors
5 bells, from Los Angeles County
I.N.S. Woman's Club of Briggs
1 bell
Section, El Camino Real Association
1 bell

The above lists are similar, but their differences reveal a significant struggle within the county about bell placement.

In April 1909, the Ventura Tuesday Club prepared a Bell Garden and placed a bell in the triangle park in front of the Thompson Lumber Company at the corner of Thompson and Front streets. Other cities and towns in Ventura County lost no time in challenging restrictions on the erection of these bell guideposts. Simi, Moorpark, and Santa Paula all laid claim to having been, at one time or another, along El Camino Real and felt that they were entitled to have a bell. Even the Ventura County Board of Supervisors was charged with placing a bell on the wrong road.

In true partisan form, Mrs. M. E. Dudley, member of the state committee of the El Camino Real Association, defended the established route by explaining:

> I understand the wish of some of our citizens is to place the Bell sign posts . . . along the road through Santa Paula, Camulos, and Newhall etc. This can never be done as the name "El Camino Real" is protected by copyright. These bells can not be placed except along the regularly laid out and officially accepted El Camino Real. . . . the following facts of history will tell you briefly why it was located by Conejo pass and not by way of Camulos and Newhall. . . . Mr. Del Valle was a member of the committee who located the road via Conejo and voted for the road as it now runs. He stated that the Camulos had only a horse trail until after Gen. Fremont built the road.

Another factor in the selection of the Conejo route was (following the original intention of the project) the "line" connecting the missions: Mission San Gabriel (1771); Los Angeles Pueblo (1781); Mission San Buenaventura (1782); and Mission San Fernando (1797). Travel between these missions went from Mission San Gabriel via Los Angeles and Cahuenga and

*El Camino Real
bell in front of the
Ventura City Hall.*

Conejo passes through San Buenaventura for fifteen years
before Mission San Fernando was founded. When Mission
San Fernando was first established, it was located on the
lower part of Encino Rancho, situated directly on the road
leading from Los Angeles Pueblo to Mission San
Buenaventura. Later it was moved to its present site and
immediately a road began to lead from Cahuenga Pass to the
new Mission San Fernando and back again to the Encino
Rancho and on to San Buenaventura.

Ventura County still holds proudly to the history of
Mission San Buenaventura, and to the ranchos, trails, pio-
neer families, and their descendants. It continues to recog-
nize the importance of keeping that history alive. Ventura
County can boast of more than twenty-four bells along El
Camino Real and in other locations throughout the county.
In 1964, a bell provided by the Native Daughters of the
Golden West was erected in front of the Ventura County
Courthouse, now the Ventura City Hall.

❧ The Dedicated Women of California ❧

On looking back over the past century, several names leap out of the history of this most noteworthy venture. The salvation and commemoration of El Camino Real and its familiar green bells are inextricably entwined with the names of the women who worked so tirelessly to ensure the success of the project. Miss Anna Pitcher, Mrs. A. S. C. Forbes, and Mrs. Eileen Dismuke speak to us from the past. Now, as we enter the new millennium, another name is added to that impressive list, Mrs. Maureen Everett. Each gave to the fullest of her time and talent to rally the support of the thousands of women whose efforts ensured the success of the project.

The Committee for El Camino Real, like the El Camino Real Association, no longer exists, having for the present fulfilled its purpose. Only long and dedicated work, primarily by women, made these organizations and their successes possible. Charles Lummis recognized their contribution in these comments:

> And there are the Women's Clubs—a truly remarkable host in Southern California; remarkable not only for number, not only for membership, but perhaps most of all for vitality. There is no hazard in remarking that any one of the most prominent of these Women's Clubs in this region is doing more to keep alive the flame of intellectuality than all the men's clubs put together. That is doubtless a truism for the whole country.[39]

And as CFWC past-president Sandy Morgan so aptly put it, they are " . . . Rich in the Traditions of the Past, Aware of the Needs of the Present, and Committed to the Challenges of the Future." These women and the California Federation of Women's Clubs will be always remembered for their service. When the history of the CFWC in the twentieth century is written, the ambitious project of preserving the oldest and most famous roadway in California will take its place with the other noble causes of these dedicated ladies, such as lobbying for child labor laws, abolishing sweat shops, and establishing schools, hospitals, and libraries. Their Adopt-A-Bell project will live in California history.

39. *Outwest* (1910), p. 82.

APPENDIX

ഇൾ

The Route of El Camino Real, circa 1900

ഇൾ

American Automobile Association Strip Maps
of El Camino Real, 1912

ഇൾ

Generations of El Camino Real Bells

ഇൾ

Donors and Locations of Bells

ഇൾ

Bells Donated by the California Federation of
Women's Clubs

ഇൾ

Biographies
Mrs. A. S. C. Forbes
Justin Kramer

The Route of El Camino Real, circa 1900

Names in bold are at the end of a branch of El Camino Real.

Mission San Diego, Old Town, Rose Canyon, Del Mar

The road divides to
Oceanside, Mission San Juan Capistrano, Myford-Irving, Tustin, Santa Ana, Orange, Anaheim, Fullerton, La Habra, Whittier, Mission San Gabriel

or to
Mission San Luis Rey, **Pala**

The road divides to
Los Angeles, Hollywood, Cahuenga Pass, Sherman Way

or to
(Camino Real de San Bernardino)
El Monte, La Puente, Pomona, Claremont, Upland, Cucamonga, Etiwanda, San Bernardino, Redlands, **Colton**

The road divides to
Calabasas, Camarillo, Mission San Buenaventura, Mission Santa Barbara, Gaviota, Mission Santa Ynez, Mission La Purisima, Los Olivos, Santa Maria, Mission San Luis Obispo, Paso Robles, Mission San Miguel, Jolon, Mission San Antonio de Padua, Ruins of Mission Soledad, Salinas

or to
(El Camino Real San Fernando)
Mission San Fernando

The road divides to
Mission San Juan Bautista, San Jose

or to
Monterey,
Mission Carmel

The road divides to
Santa Clara, Palo Alto, Redwood City, San Mateo, Colma, Hayward, Ocean View, Mission de los Dolores

or to
(Camino Real de San Jose)
Mission San Jose, San Leandro, Oakland, San Pablo, **Mission San Rafael**

or to
Benicia, **Mission San Francisco Solana de Sonoma**

The road divides to
San Francisco water front, from the water front by water to Mission San Rafael, **Mission San Francisco Solano de Sonoma**

or to
San Francisco Presidio

American Automobile Association Strip Maps of El Camino Real, 1912

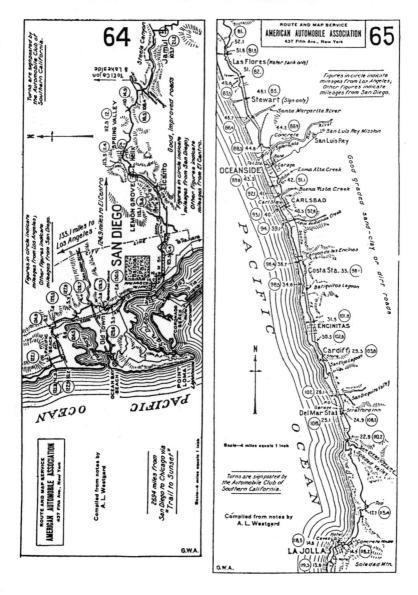

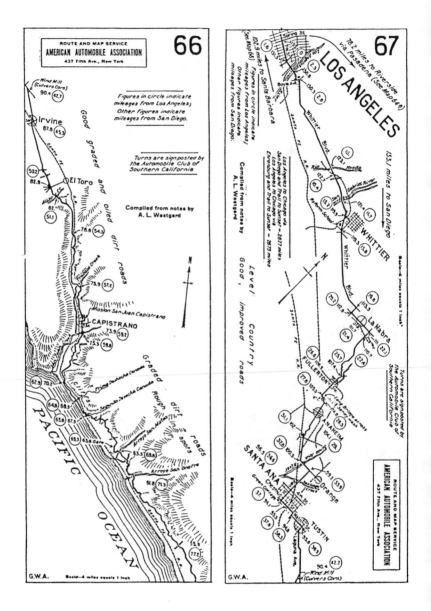

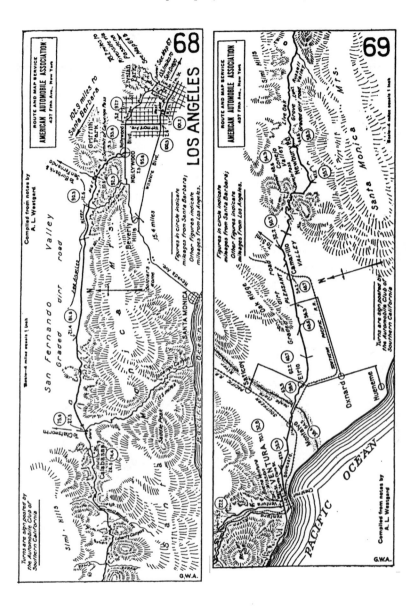

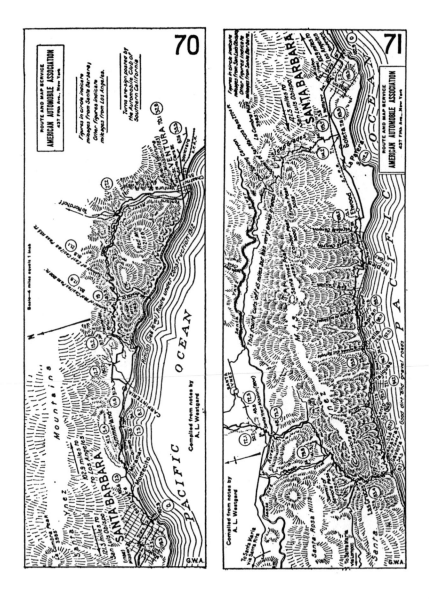

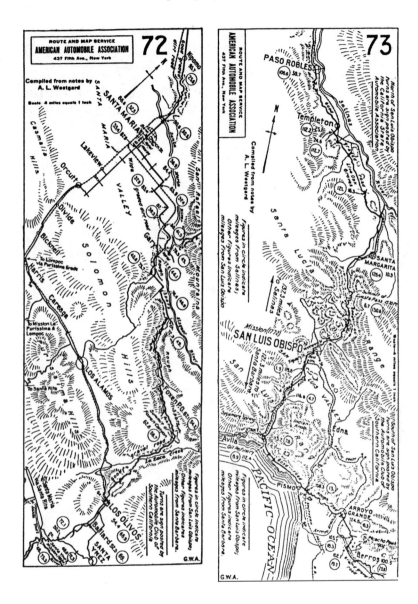

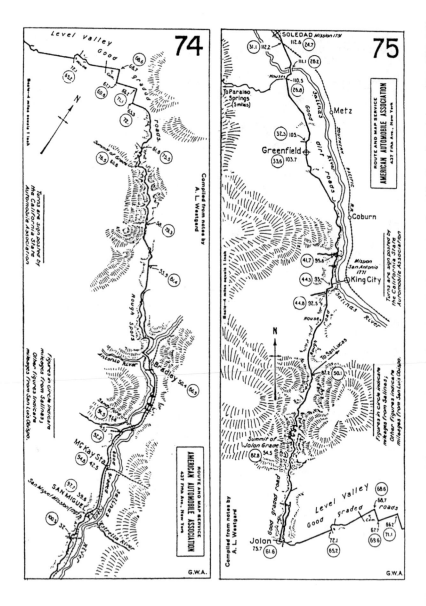

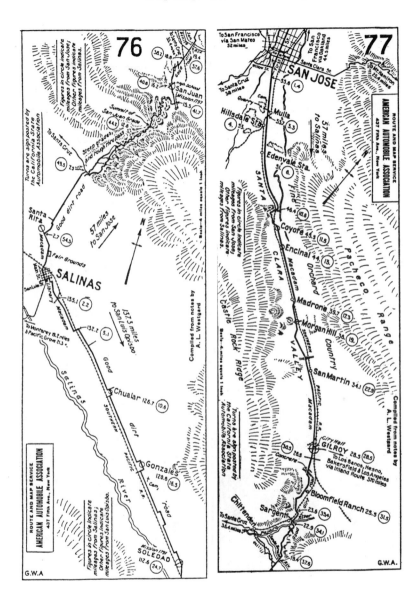

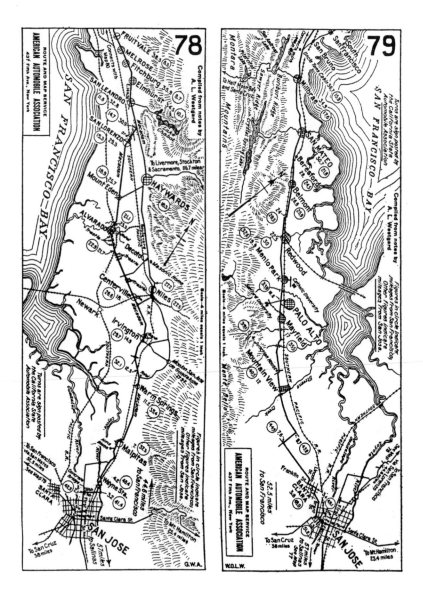

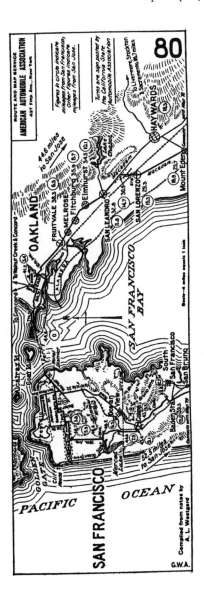

Generations of El Camino Real Bells

From 1906, when the first bell was installed, to the end of the twentieth century, there have been fifteen generations of bells, made in three different styles.

Mrs. Forbes had her own style, which were made from 1906 to 1948. It has distinctive markings on the bell body (Nos. 1 through 5).

When Caltrans was requested to provide bells (circa 1957) they designed a flat top bell that was cast in a foundry in Fresno, California, and represented a very distinct design (Nos. 6 and 7).

During late 1950s, Justin Kramer was awarded the contract to cast bells for Caltrans. His basic design is shown as generation No. 8. Sometime during the period 1960–1965, bells started showing up on the highways that were similar to Kramer's bell, but with a different inscription. We have no knowledge of the name of this foundry, only that it was contracted by the state of California (Nos. 9, 10, 11, and 12).

When the bells became expensive, in excess of $100, Caltrans looked for a more economical style. They found it in a concrete bell. In fact, they now have two styles of concrete bells. Using the flat top (No. 6) as a pattern, they made a concrete replica (No. 14). Using Kramer's bell (No. 8) as a pattern, they made a second concrete bell (No. 13).

The latest generation to be placed on El Camino Real is the only variation that Mr. Kramer has made since he started casting El Camino Real bells. This was in 1997 when the legend was changed to create the International El Camino Real bell (No. 15).

The following are characteristics of each type of bell:

1. ORIGINAL BELL DESIGN

The original design by Mrs. A. S. C. Forbes bore the familiar dates of 1769–1906 at the waist of the bell. Along the lip directly below the dates are the words *El Camino Real*. Along the lip, 180 degrees from the front wording, is *Patented and copyright 1906 by Mrs. A. S. C. Forbes*. This bell was the only type to be fitted with a clapper. The bands around the waist are the familiar marks identifying these bells as being cast by Forbes. When this bell was first placed, it was not painted,

exposing the bare iron to the elements. The mounting pad can have one, two, or three holes. The bell's weight is approximately ninety-two pounds and it measures eighteen inches high by eighteen inches in diameter. Numerous original bells are still to be found at locations along El Camino Real, city and county roads, and at various missions.

2. SECOND GENERATION

Strikingly similar to the original, this bell lacks the copyright statement, Mrs. Forbes's name, and a clapper. The dates are the same as on the original bell and the weight, size, and material are also the same. There are quite a few of these bells at various locations throughout the state on El Camino Real and at other public sites.

3. PLAIN BELL, NO LEGEND

This bell is the same basic shape and size as the first- and second-generation bells but it was cast without any legend. These bells are located mainly in the San Diego area.

4. LANDMARK BELL

On this bell the word *Landmark* replaced the dates 1769–1906, but the legend on the lip remained El Camino Real. This bell, also cast of iron, was to be installed at three inland locations. It can be assumed that this bell is similar to the original and second-generation bells. It seems the landmark bell was ordered for locations not on or along El

Camino Real. The 1914 El Camino Real Association's annual report by Mrs. Forbes shows that only three of these bells were installed.

5. EL CAMINO REAL ASSO-CIATION BELL

Similar to the original and second-generation bells but lacking the copyright statement and clapper. Below the dates 1769–1906 and around the lip are the words *El Camino Real Assn.* There are no records to explain when or why these bells were cast. What few of these bells have been located are found around the San Jose area. The weight, size, and material are the same as the original bell.

6. STATE OF CALIFOR-NIA BELL

On September 17, 1974, the California Department of Transportation contracted for 50 bells of a very unusual design, featuring a flat crown and right-angle shoulders with the words *Property of the State of California* cast in a circle onto the flat top. This bell had the dates

1769–1906 around the waist and *El Camino Real* around the lip directly below the dates. These bells proved to be costly and were discontinued in favor of a design more easily cast and "more bell-like in design." Its dimensions are seventeen inches high by fifteen inches in diameter.

7. STATE OF CALIFORNIA BELL, DOUBLE-DATED BELL

These bells are the same design as No. 6 above, with its smooth sides and lack of the copyright legend. This bell has a duplicate set of dates and El Camino Real legends, locat-

ed 180 degrees apart. The dates 1769–1906 are located on the waist and the words *El Camino Real* are located on the lip below the dates. This bell is eighteen inches high by eighteen inches in diameter. Its weight is approximately ninety pounds.

8. JUSTIN KRAMER BELL, STANDARD DESIGN

These bells can be identified by the absence of bands around the body of the bell, smooth sides, rounded shoulders, and large lip band. The dates 1769–1906 are located on the waist and the words *El Camino Real* are located on the lip below the dates. This bell is eighteen inches high by eighteen inches in diameter with a weight of approximately ninety pounds. This was the most popular design from 1960 until 1996.

9. STATE OF CALIFORNIA BELL, LETTERING INSIDE OF RIM

These can be identified by the smooth waist area, absence of bands around the body of the bell, and the absence of a copyright legend. These bells are made unique by the legend cast on the inside rim that reads *Property of the*

State of California. The dates 1769–1906 are located on the waist with the words *El Camino Real* located on the lip below the dates. The size and weight of this bell is unknown.

10. STATE OF CALIFORNIA BELL, DOUBLE-DATED BELL
This bell was contracted by the California Department of Transportation. The dates 1769–1906 on the body and the words *El Camino Real* on the lip appear on each side of the bell, opposite each other, thus creating a double-dated bell. There are only a few of these bells, most being found in northern and central California. Its dimensions are seventeen inches high by fifteen inches in diameter.

11. STATE OF CALIFORNIA BELL, RAISED LETTERING ON SHOULDER
This bell can be identified by the absence of bands around the body. It has smooth sides and lacks the copyright legend. Around the shoulder is raised lettering in a circle that can only be read when looking down on the top. The lettering reads *Property of the State of California.* The dates 1769–1906 are located on the waist and the words *El Camino Real* are located on the lip below the dates. This bell is eighteen inches high by eighteen inches in diameter, and weighs approximately ninety pounds. Only one is known to exist. It is located in the California State Capital Museum in Sacramento.

12. STATE OF CALIFORNIA BELL, RECESSED LETTERING ON SHOULDER

This bell can be identified by the absence of bands around the body. It has smooth sides and lacks the copyright legend. The crown of this bell has recessed lettering in a circle around the shoulder that can only be read when looking down on the top. The recessed lettering reads *Property of the State of California.* The dates 1769–1906 are located on the waist and the words *El Camino Real* are located on the lip below the dates. This bell is eigh-

teen inches high by eighteen inches in diameter.

13. CALTRANS CONCRETE BELL

This bell can be identified by the smooth waist area. It looks much like a Justin Kramer bell with its absence of bands around the body of the bell. This bell is unusual in that it is cast in concrete. The dates 1769–1906 are located on the waist with the words *El Camino Real* located on the lip below the dates. The size and weight of this bell is unknown.

14. CALTRANS CONCRETE BELL

This bell, first produced in 1978, is made of cast concrete, and produced by various Caltrans maintenance offices throughout California. Damaged and missing bells are replaced with this type of bell. The design is similar to No. 6, but without the inscription on the top. The words *El Camino Real* are on the rim, with the dates 1769–1906 on the waist. The bell is lighter than the iron ones, therefore less costly, and easier to transport and install. It takes about one day to set up, cast, dry, and paint this style of bell. Its dimensions are fourteen inches high by seventeen inches in diameter, with a weight of approximately forty-seven pounds.

15. INTERNATIONAL CAMINO REAL BELL

This bell is the Justin Kramer design (No. 8) with an insert at the waist (added prior to casting) containing the inscription shown here. The words *El Camino Real* are located on the lip (not shown). This bell is eighteen inches high by eighteen inches in diameter. It weighs approximately ninety pounds.

Donors and Locations of Bells

The following list is taken from annual proceedings of the Native Daughters of the Golden West, 1906–1991. Unless otherwise noted, an asterisk indicates bells donated by the Native Daughters of the Golden West and two asterisks indicate bells donated by the Native Sons of the Golden West.

Date	Donor(s)	Location
1906		
Aug. 15	N.Y. Society of California	Plaza Church, Los Angeles
August	El Camino Real Association	San Diego Mission
n.d.	NDGW	"Five Corners," Irvington
n.d.	Board of Supervisors	5 bells, locations not provided, Ventura
1907		
n.d.	Women's Clubs of Santa Paula	9 bells, locations not recorded, Ventura County
n.d.	CFWC	9 bells, locations not available
1908		
n.d.	East Whittier Improvement Club	3 bells, locations not available
n.d.	Santa Ana Ebell Club	location not available
1909		
June 15	CFWC	Mission Dolores, San Francisco
June 29	Daughters of California Pioneers	Officers Club, the Presidio, San Francisco
July 4	Dardanelle, No. 66*	forks of the road, south end of town, Sonora
Aug. 29	Monterey Woman's Civic Club	Junction of Salinas and Castroville roadway at Episcopal chapel
September	The California Club	Mission Dolores
Sept. 9	NSGW and NDGW	Hollister Avenue and Mission Street, Santa Barbara
Sept. 10	NSGW and NDGW	The fourth bell to be erected in the immediate

Date	Donor(s)	Location
1909 (cont.)		
		vicinity of San Jose, southernmost point of Cadwallader Park, First and Second Streets
Sept. 17	The California Club	Sixteenth and Dolores Streets, San Francisco
Sept. 26	El Camino, No. 144**	County road, entrance to Palo Alto
Oct. 6	Buena Ventura, No. 95*	Mission San Buenaventura
Oct. 8	Orinda, No. 56*	Howard and Sixteenth Streets, San Francisco
Oct. 17	Bonita, No. 10* Redwood Parlor No. 66*	Redwood City south outlet
Oct. 20	Redwood Parlor No. 66* Bonita, No. 10*	Redwood City
Oct. 24	Guadalupe, No. 153* NSGW, No. 231 Dolores, No. 169* NSGW, No. 208	25th Street and San Jose Avenue
Oct. 31	Calaveras, No. 103* La Estrella, No. 89* Keith, No. 137*	Kearny and Market Streets, San Francisco
Nov. 7	La Estrella, No. 89* Keith, No. 137* Calaveras, No. 103*	Market and Geary Streets, San Francisco
Nov. 14	Grand Parlor, NSGW	Portsmouth Square, San Francisco
Nov. 14	Grand Parlor, NDGW	Corner of Clay and Montgomery, San Francisco
Nov. 28	Yosemite, No. 83*	Sixteenth and Mission Streets, San Francisco
Nov. 28	San Luisita, No. 108*	Mission San Luis Obispo de Tolosa
Dec. 19	Association of Pioneer Women	Twenty-second and Dolores Streets, San Francisco
Dec. 21	City and people of San Leandro	At the plaza, Howard and San Leandro

Date	Donor(s)	Location
1909 *(cont.)*		
Dec. 26	Junípero, No. 141*	Corner Figuerora and Webster
n.d.	Grand Parlor*	Del Monte Hotel, Santa Barbara
n.d.	Grand Parlor*	Polk and California Streets, San Francisco
n.d.	NSGW Los Angeles Junípero Parlor No. 141*	Mission San Fernando
n.d.	Tuesday Club	Thompson and Front Streets, Ventura
1910		
April 3	Tamalpais*	Front of St. Raphael Catholic Church, San Rafael
April 24	Foresters of Colma	City of Colma
May	NSGW and NDGW	San Fernando Mission
May 5	Golden Era Parlor No. 99*	"Landmark" bell at Columbia
May 22	Junípero, No. 141*	Polk and Alvardo Streets, Monterey
June 16	Grand Officers NDGW	Entrance to the City on the Boulevard, foot of State Street, Santa Barbara
June 24	San Juan Bautista, No. 179*	Second and Mariposa, entrance to Arcade, San Benito County
July	Dardanelle No. 66*	"Landmark" bell at Placerville
Sept. 11	Vendome, No. 100**	Cadwallader Park, San Jose
n.d.	Improvement Club*	Mission San Buenaventura
n.d.	Cabrillo Parlor*	Ventura Ave., two blocks from Mission
n.d.	Ladies Club of Ventura	Foster Park at the stone bridge
n.d.	Pioneer Society of Ventura	County line at Los Angeles
n.d.	Pioneer Society of Ventura	County line at Santa Barbara

Date	Donor(s)	Location
1911		
Feb. 5	ECRA, Los Angeles Section	Adelheid Baths, South Los Angeles Street near Broadway
July 4	Dardanelle, No. 66*	not recorded
Oct. 2	Oro Fino, No. 9*	San Jose Avenue and San Francisco County line
n.d.	CFWC Southern District Arrowhead Parlor No. 149* Arrowhead Parlor No. 110**	Seventeen bells in San Gabriel Mission Chapel, San Bernardino
n.d.	Las Lamas, No. 72*	Dolores Street near Seventeenth, San Francisco
n.d.	Orinda, No. 56* Buena Vista, No. 56* Golden State, No. 68* Fremont, No. 50* Darina No. 114* Gabrielle, No. 139* Presidio, No. 148*	Howard and Fifteenth Streets, San Francisco
1912		
Dec. 5	Grand Parlor, NDGW	Mission San Antonio de Padua
n.d.	Placerville Women's Club	Old El Dorado Trail to Colma
n.d.	Monday Afternoon Club Corvina	not recorded
n.d.	California Badger Club	not recorded
n.d.	Gentlemen's Club of Upland	not recorded
1913		
March 26	La Estrella, No. 89*	Mission and Fifteenth Streets, San Francisco
Dec. 14	Escholtzia Chapter, DAR	Los Angeles City
1914		
n.d.	Dr. M. Kibbe Alameda Club women Alameda County Supervisors	8 bells, locations not recorded
n.d.	San Miguel, No. 94* San Miguel, No. 150**	Mission San Miguel
1915		
May 15	Grand Parlor, NDGW	Eighth and Broadway, Oakland

Date	Donor(s)	Location
1915 *(cont.)*		
n.d.	Corvina Chapter, DAR	one mile south of San Juan Capistrano
1916		
Nov. 13	Pioneer Society of Los Angeles	San Fernando and Sunset Boulevard, Los Angeles
n.d.	NDGW Grand Parlor	Colton Hall, Monterey
n.d.	DAR of Los Angeles	Los Angeles city/county
1917		
July	DAR of San Francisco	Mission Carmel
1919		
n.d.	DAR of Los Angeles	two miles south of San Juan Capistrano
1939		
March 17	Topanga, No. 269*	Santa Susana Pass
Aug. 3	NSGW and NDGW	Dunning and Mills Roads, Ventura
1947		
n.d.	Automobile Club of Southern California	Lankershim Boulevard, Los Angeles
1953		
May 2	Topanga, No. 269*	Calabasas Adobe, Los Angeles
1959		
n.d.	La Tijera, No. 282*	Pacific Coast Highway, San Diego
n.d.	Children/American Revolution	Pacific Coast Highway, San Diego
1962		
n.d.	Presidio, No. 148	Millbrae
1963		
August	Mr. and Mrs. G. Whitney	Petra, Majorca, Spain
December	Marinita, No. 198*	Jack London Square, Oakland
1964		
Aug	El Aliso, No. 314*	Rancho Camulos, Ventura
1965		
Feb. 28	Tierra de Oro, No. 304	Santa Barbara Historical Society

Date	Donor(s)	Location
1965 (*cont.*)		
May	Ventura County Museum	Mission San Buena-ventura
Dec. 4	Tierra de Oro, No. 304*	Santa Barbara Court House
n.d.	San Ysidro Woman's Club	San Ysidro police station
1966		
April 22	Lugenia, No. 241*	San Bernardino County Museum
Sept. 24	Rudecinda, No. 230*	Mission San Diego chapel entrance
Sept. 24	Mission Bell, No. 316*	Mission Soledad, mission grounds,
Sept. 24	Grand Parlor, NDGW	Crossroads to mission, San Diego
Nov. 19	Belmont Woman's Club	City of Belmont
Dec. 10	Poppy Trail, No. 266*	City of Montebello
n.d.	CFWC	North of La Jolla
1967		
May 20	Placerita, No. 277*	Leonis Adobe–Calabasas Road, Los Angeles
Nov. 19	Belmont Woman's Club	location not reported
1968		
March 12	Junípero, No. 141*	Carmel Mission divider
n.d.	Placerita, No. 277*	Crespi High School, Encino
1969		
Feb.	Placerita, No. 277*	United California Bank (UCB), Encino
1971		
Jan 29	San Jose, No. 81*	UCB Sunnyvale
April 21	Reina del Mar, No. 126* Tierra de Oro, No. 304	UCB, 901 State Street, Santa Barbara
April 29	Poinsettia, No. 318*	UCB, Westlake Village
June 3	Poinsettia, No. 318*	UCB, Camarillo
July	NDGW	UCB, San Diego
Dec. 3	Reina del Mar, No. 126* Tierra de Oro, No. 304*	UCB, State Street, Santa Barbara
n.d.	NDGW	UCB, San Gabriel
n.d.	NDGW	City Hall mall, Thousand Oaks

Date	Donor(s)	Location
1972		
n.d.	Cien Anos, No. 303*	Saddleback Inn, Norwalk
n.d.	La Bandera, No. 110*	UCB, Los Angeles
1974		
Sept.	Poinsetta No. 318*	Olivas adobe, Ventura
Sept. 18	San Juan Bautista, No. 179*	Rededication, Mission San Juan Bautista
1985		
Nov. 2	Anaheim Historical Society Anaheim Museum	Carnegie Library
Nov. 2	Anaheim Historical Society Anaheim Museum	White Horse restaurant, Anaheim Boulevard
n.d.	Tierra de Oro, No. 304*	Dismuke residence, Santa Barbara
1991		
June 18	NDGW	Valley Forge, Pennsylvania
1997		
Jan. 29	CFWC Woman's Club of Escondido	Grape Day Park, Escondido
April 9	CFWC Woman's Club of Vista	Rancho Guajome, Vista
May 28	CFWC Mountain View Woman's Club	El Camino and Castro Streets, Los Altos
Sept. 11	Mrs. Hanna Betcone	Rededication, Oceania, San Diego
Sept. 27	Torrance Woman's Club	Sepulveda Boulevard east of Camino Real
Oct. 25	Sister City, Hermosa Beach CFWC Associaton	Loreto, Baja California Sur
Nov. 15	CFWC San Diego District No. 25 CFWC Allied Gardens Woman's Club CFWC Clairemont Woman's Club CFWC Mission Beach Woman's Club CFWC Peninsula Woman's Club CFWC San Diego Woman's Club CFWC Tierrasanta Woman's Club	Mission Trails Regional Park
1998		
March	Palo Alto Historical Association and CFWC Iranian Woman's Club	Location not reported

Date	Donor(s)	Location
1998 (cont.)		
March	CFWC Iranian Woman's Club	Location not reported
June 6	CFWC Julian Woman's Club	Santa Ysabel
June 22	California Federation of Women's Clubs	Border between San Diego and Tijuana
March 20	CWFC Rancho Temecula Area Women's Club	Temecula Museum
1999		
Feb. 16	San Diego Mission Bells Chapter of the American Bell Association (rededicated). Daughters of the American Colonists placed the original bell.	Camp Pendleton
n.d.	Caltrans, District 11	Caltrans office, San Diego
n.d.	California Federation of Women's Clubs	Perry's Restaurant, Pacific Coast Highway and Taylor Streets, San Diego

Bells Donated by the California Federation of Women's Clubs

The following CFWC districts and clubs have erected one or more bells on El Camino Real from 1996 to 1999, as reported by the Adopt-A-Bell project office.

Redwood District No. 1

Redwood District

Shasta District No. 4

Shasta District

Sutter District No. 5

CFWC Cool Study Club
Sutter District (2)

Golden Gate District No. 6

Belmont Federated Women's Club (4)
Golden Gate District
Philippine Association of University Women
Redwood City Women's Club
South San Francisco Women's Club (2)

Alameda District No. 7

Alta Mira Club
Hill and Valley Women's Club
Montclair Woman's Club

Mount Diablo District No. 8

Alamo Women's Club
Clayton Woman's Club
Lafayette, Moraga, and Orinda Jr. Women's Clubs
Women's Club of Martinez
Women's Club of Dublin
Tracy Women's Club
Orinda Women's Club
Mt. Diablo District

Loma Prieta District No. 9

Country Women's Club of Campbell
Cupertino Federated Women's Club
Iranian Woman's Club (2)
Mountain View Woman's Club

Peninsula Hills Women's Club
Santa Clara Woman's Club (3)
Santa Cruz Women's Club
West Valley Federated Women's Club
Women's Club of Hollister
Loma Prieta District

Fresno District No. 11

Fig Garden Woman's Club
Kingsburg Tuesday Club
Reedley Study and Civic Club

Sequoia District No. 12

Porterville Women's Club
Sequoia District

Kern District No. 13

Kern District (2)
Wasco Women's Club

Tierra Adorada District No. 14

Alpha Literary and Improvement Club
Camarillo Women's Club
Conejo Valley Woman's Club
Ladies in Leadership
El Camino Women's Club
Moorpark Fortnightly Women's Club
Morro Bay Women's Club
Oak View Women's Club
Santa Maria Community Club
San Buenaventura Women's Club
Simi Valley Women's Club (2)
Tierra Adorada District (5)
Town and Country Women's Club of Santa Barbara
Women's Service Club of Goleta

Sierra Cahuenga District No. 15

Rosamond Women's Club
Fallbrook Women's Club
Sierra Cahuenga District
Woodland Hills Women's Club
Woman's Club of Burbank

Verdugo-Metropolitan Districts No. 16/17

Los Angeles Philippine Women's Club

Pasadena Women's Club
Sierra Madre Women's Club
Sunland Woman's Club

Marina District No. 18

Marina District
Culver City Women's Club
Mar Vista Women's Club
Torrance Women's Club

San Gabriel Valley District No. 20

Baldwin Park Women's Club
Baldwin Park Junior Women's Club
Hacienda Heights Women's Club
Montebello Women's Club
Monterey Park Women's Club
Monterey Park Junior Women's Club
San Gabriel Valley District
San Gabriel Women's Club
Santa Fe Springs Women's Club
Women's Club of West Covina

San Bernardino District No. 21

Chino Valley Women's Club
Contemporary Club, Redlands
Grand Terrace Women's club
Rancho Cucamonga Woman's Club
San Bernardino District
San Bernardino District Juniors
Women's Club of Rialto

Orange District No. 22

Ebell Club of Anaheim
El Camino Real Junior Women's Club
Fountain Valley Women's Club
CFWC Canyon Hills Juniors
Orange District Juniors
Rancho Viejo Juniors
San Clemente Juniors
Tustin Area Woman's Club

De Anza District No. 23

De Anza District
Rancho-Temecula Area Women's Club

Palomar District No. 24

Bonsall Women's Club
Fallbrook Women's Club
Julian Women's Club (2)
San Dieguito Women's Club
Women's Club of Vista (2)

San Diego District No. 25

Allied Gardens Women's Club
Clairemont Women's Club (2)
Mira Mesa Junior Women's Club
Mission Beach Women's Club
Pacific Beach Women's Club
Past Presidents Association, San Diego
Peninsula Women's Club
San Diego Women's Club (2)
San Diego District (3)
Tierrasanta Women's Club

Southern District No. 26

Bostonia Women's Club
El Cajon Women's Club
Rolando Woman's Club
San Ysidro Women's Club
Sweetwater Women's Club
Women's Club of Lakeside

California Federation of Women's Clubs (4)

Biographies

Mrs. A. S. C. Forbes

The woman whose outstanding work contributed most to the marking of El Camino Real in the early part of the twentieth century was, of course, Mrs. A. S. C. Forbes. She was born Harrye Rebecca Piper Smith, of Quaker parents in Everett, Pennsylvania, May 6, 1861. The first of six children, her early years are a mystery. At some point she moved with her family to Wichita, Kansas, where she attended a private college in 1883. The school closed early in 1884.

In 1886 we find a marriage license issued to A. S. C. Forbes and Harrye Piper Smith. This marriage would seem to have been quite remarkable. Both were energetic, industrious, high achievers, as evidenced by their accomplishments, both singly and jointly, over the years.

In addition to owning a large herd of cattle, Forbes was owner of the Pacific Bottling Works in Tacoma, Washington, during 1890-1891. This company had a corner on the market for all bottled soft drinks sold in the Pacific Northwest and Alaska. He sold this business in 1891 and moved with his young wife to London.

While in England, Forbes was proprietor of the Blair Camera Company, which had factories in Boston, Massachusetts, and Pawtucket, Rhode Island, and warehouses in London. In addition to camera equipment, this company made the first rollable film. He sold the business to the Kodak Company in 1897.

In England Mrs. Forbes is said to have attended the Heatherly Art School in London, but no records can be found to substantiate this. While in Europe, she and her husband lived in Spain for an unknown period of time before returning to the United States. After landing in New York they took the train cross-country to California, where they settled in Los Angeles in 1895.

In 1900 Armitage Suton Carion Forbes became a citizen of the United States. Like his wife, he was a member of numerous civic organizations and the Los Angeles Chamber of Commerce. He also found time to go big game hunting with the world famous hunter and adventurer, Paul Du Chaillu. Among his many and varied activities, he owned a gypsum company, a photo manufacturing company in Los Angeles, and an orange grove in Glendora, and was part owner of a gold mine in Kern County. He also dealt in real estate in Los Angeles. An expert photographer, his work won honors in the salons of London, San Francisco, and Los Angeles.

The Forbeses settled into a busy life in their new home, becoming involved in community affairs and playing active roles in many civic organizations. Mrs. Forbes worked as a freelance reporter for an eastern newspaper. Her work was widely read across the country, in much the same way as syndication works today.

In response to a request from her publisher for something unique for Memorial Day, she wrote of an old Chinese tradition of floating flowers on the waters to honor the memory of departed loved ones. Consequently, Mrs. Forbes was honored by the Secretary of the Navy for her role in establishing the custom of casting flowers on the waters to remember departed friends.

> Thanks to the indefatigable labors of Mrs. A. S. C. Forbes of Los Angeles, the beautiful ceremony of strewing flowers on the restless ocean waters in honor of the naval dead was first observed at Santa Monica on Memorial Day in 1900, and bids to become an appropriate national custom.[40]

In 1901 she was named to the board of directors of the Los Angeles Camera Club and was an exhibitor at the first Los Angeles Photographic Salon.

The year 1902 proved to be quite eventful for this lady of boundless energy. She was appointed director at large for the Los Angeles Camera Club, made chair of the salon committee, and opened the first photographic salon in Los Angeles. She was also named to be the first state chair of the California History and Landmarks Department of the state Federation of Women's Clubs.[41] She served in this capacity until 1906.

40. H. Newark, *Sixty Years in Southern California* (New York: Knickerbocker Press, 1916), p. 621.

41. Not to be confused with the California Landmarks and History Club, which Mrs. Forbes organized in 1916. She served as president from that date until May of 1925.

Mrs. A. S. C. Forbes "casting flowers on the waves," circa 1900.

Mrs. Forbes always had a passion for history and found in California's rich and colorful Hispanic heritage a bountiful source of inspiration for her nimble mind and camera lens. She visited the missions and made photos depicting Native Americans and their customs. She also studied the bells of the missions, sketching them and learning about the processes used in producing them. She professed a love for and fascination with bells.

When the El Camino Real Association was formed in 1904, she served on the executive committee, as well as filling the role of auditor, and later served as president. During this time she designed the bell and standard that would be adopted by the committee as the appropriate and enduring marker for El Camino Real.

At some point after 1908, the Forbeses acquired a foundry and began producing El Camino Real bells. In 1914 they started the Novelty Manufacturing Company of Los Angeles, where they made miniature Camino Real bells and mission bells, as well as road markers and an assortment of large bells which were shipped all over the country and overseas.

While searching through library archives, Mrs. Forbes came across the long-lost Treaty of Cahuenga which was signed by General Andrés Pico and Lieutenant Colonel John C. Frémont on January 13, 1847, ending hostilities between Mexico and California. She then worked tirelessly to gather proof of the location of the site where the treaty was signed, Campo de Cahuenga, and have it declared a memorial park. And so it stands today, a tribute to the drive and persistence of one determined woman.

In 1928, on the death of her husband, Mrs. Forbes took over the operation of the foundry, at times even donning an apron and taking a hand in the work herself. It has been claimed that she was the only foundry-woman in the world at that time. There is evidence that one of her brothers, most likely John Luther Smith, helped her run the business after her husband's death. She continued making bells until 1948 when she sold the California Bell Company because of ill health.

During her busy life in Los Angeles, she found time to write four books, *Los Angeles, Official Guide* (1903), *Mission Tales in the Days of the Dons* (1909), *California Missions and Landmarks* (1914), and *The Little Shepherds of Bethlehem*, as well as many newspaper articles. She was a member of the CFWC, D.A.R., and an honorary member of The Native Daughters of the Golden West, as well as Navy Post 278 of the American Legion.

On September 18, 1951, Mrs. A. S. C. Forbes passed away in Los Angeles after a long and extremely productive life. She left a mark on California history in more than one way. Her memory was honored with a plaque dedicated at Campo de Cahuenga in 1952. It reads:

HONORING THE MEMORY OF
MRS. ARMITAGE S. C. FORBES
Historian, Author and Civic Leader,
Through whose Devotion to the History of California
This Site of the Signing of the Treaty of Cahuenga
Jan. 13, 1847
Was Preserved For Ever.
Placed by Campo de Cahuenga Memorial Association of
California in 1952

Justin Kramer

Justin Kramer is a name well known to the many organizations involved with El Camino Real bells. For nearly forty years he has been casting the historic markers placed along California's most celebrated roadway.

Kramer's father had lived in Ventura as a boy at the time the first El Camino Real bell marker was placed in front of the Plaza Church in Los Angeles. After completing his Navy service during World War I, his father, a historian specializing in California history, fulfilled a life-long dream by moving the family to California in 1929.

Kramer attended the University of Southern California, graduating with honors at age nineteen. After graduation, he continued his studies, earning the degree of master of music. While a student, he worked as a musician in all the major motion picture studios in the Los Angeles area. His interest in bells was a natural extension of his interest in both music and physics, and much of his life has been associated with "musical acoustics." A pipe organ builder, he was a member of the International Society of Organ Builders and is presently a member of the Audio Engineering Society and the American Guild of Organists. He has been awarded around twenty U.S. patents for his inventions. He served as special consultant to the University of California in the construction of the famous bell towers at the Riverside and Santa Barbara campuses, and he has worked with many architects in the design of bell towers.

It was his knowledge of bells that lead to being commissioned by the Mission Trails Association in 1962 to produce a bell profile to replace bells along El Camino Real. His work here has included the production of over four hundred such bells. His most recent contribution is the design and casting of the newest generation of the bell, the international bell. This special bell has, thus far, been placed in three different locations in Baja California, marking the trail of the padres as El Camino Real Misionero. More are planned.

Kramer is the author of *Cast in America: The Historically Accurate, Exciting Story of the Liberty Bell*, a project which combined his expertise in music and physics with his love of

El Camino Real

Jean & Justin Kramer

history. In it he dispells many of the myths that surround one of our nation's most revered symbols.

Kramer and his wife Jean currently make their home in Huntington Beach, California. The pair composed an origi-

nal song to commemorate El Camino Real, which has been chosen as the official song of the Adopt-A-Bell project of the CFWC.

Travel With Someone You Trust®

Whenever you go, it's good to have a guide. Someone who knows the territory. Someone who can help you find those hidden spots and great deals. For generations of travelers, AAA has been that guide.

When you join AAA, you gain access to a world of information: AAA TourBooks, TripTiks, and maps help you find exciting things to do and wonderful places to stay. As a member of one of the world's largest consumer organizations, you receive the best deals from the world's best travel providers as well as valuable discounts from a wide range of Show Your Card and Save® partners. In additions, AAA financial and insurance services provide the freedom to help you pay for your travels and enjoy peace of mind on the ride.

As a AAA member, you join a community that numbers over 42 million members and that provides partnerships with the biggest names in travel. As part of our ongoing involvement with community affairs, AAA has had a long history of involvement with many diverse public service programs including, for example, the Mission Bell Trail Markers and the historic recognition of El Camino Real. As far back as 1919, the California State Automobile Association endorsed a campaign to raise funds to restore the Missions and in 1921, the Automobile Club of Southern California and the California State Automobile Association took over, for more than a decade, the actual maintenance of the Mission Bell Trail Markers. This tradition continues today in more recent campaigns conducted in cooperation with the California Federation of Women's Clubs.

We invite you to explore the world. Let AAA be your guide. With over 4,000 offices nationwide, you can find us in many local communities or on the Web at www.aaa.com.